TIME® Writer's Notebook
Level D
Copyright © 2006
Time Inc.

TIME and the Red Border Design are registered trademarks of Time Inc. All rights reserved. Developed in collaboration with Exploring Writing and distributed by Teacher Created Materials Publishing.

TIME Learning Ventures
Editorial Director: Keith GartonProject Editor: The Quarasan Group, Inc.Design Production: The Quarasan Group, Inc. Illustrator: The Quarasan Group, Inc.Teacher Reviewers: Michele Acosta, IL; Laura Clark, IL; Brian Glassman, MD; Nancy Kern, VA; Mary Lou Kinsella, IL; Jennifer Lozier, IL; Jana Miller, TX; Susan Romberg, IL

Exploring Wr
© 2005 by Teac

Teacher Created Materials Publishing
Publisher: Rachelle Cracchiolo, M.S. Ed.
Editor-in-Chief: Sharon Coan, M.S. Ed.
Editorial Director: Dona Herweck Rice

ISBN: 978-0-7439-0377-6

Teacher Created Materials
5301 Oceanus Drive
Huntington Beach, CA 92649-1030
http://www.tcmpub.com
Reprinted 2012

Photography credits:
p. 5: (t) PhotoDisc, Inc., (c) PhotoDisc, Inc., (b) PhotoDisc, Inc.; p. 7: PhotoDisc, Inc.; p. 9: Comstock; p. 11. Comstock; p. 12: Artville LLC; p. 13: Comstock; p. 17: ImageClub; p. 18: MetaCreations/Kai Power Photos; p. 19: Artville; p. 20: (t) PhotoDisc, Inc., (b) PhotoDisc, Inc.; p. 21: PhotoDisc, Inc.; p. 23: Comstock, p. 25: (t) PhotoDisc, Inc., (c) PhotoDisc, Inc., (b) PhotoDisc, Inc.; p. 26: Comstock; p. 27: Corel; p. 29: Comstock; p. 30: Comstock; p. 36: Comstock; p. 43: (t) PhotoDisc, Inc., (c) PhotoDisc, Inc., (b) PhotoDisc, Inc.; p. 45: Comstock; p. 46: PhotoDisc, Inc.; p. 49: PhotoDisc, Inc.; p. 50: Corbis; p. 53: (t) PhotoDisc, Inc., (l) PhotoDisc, Inc., (c) PhotoDisc, Inc., (r) PhotoDisc, Inc.; p. 55: PhotoDisc, Inc.; p. 56: PhotoDisc, Inc.; p. 58: (t) PhotoDisc, Inc., (b) MetaCreations/Kai Power Photos; p. 61: PhotoDisc, Inc.; p. 62: PhotoDisc, Inc.; p. 67: (t) PhotoDisc, Inc., (c) MetaCreations/Kai Power Photos; p. 68: Corbis; p. 69: Corbis; pp. 70–71: Corbis; pp. 72–75: PhotoDisc, Inc.; p. 76: (t) PhotoDisc, Inc., (b) PhotoDisc, Inc.; p. 77: Artville; p. 78: Artville LLC; p. 81: PhotoDisc, Inc.; p. 93: (t) PhotoDisc, Inc., (bkgnd.) PhotoDisc, Inc., (c) PhotoDisc, Inc., (l) PhotoDisc, Inc.; p. 94: Comstock; p. 96: Artville LLC; pp. 99–100: PhotoDisc, Inc.; p. 102: PhotoDisc, Inc.; p. 104: PhotoDisc, Inc.; pp. 108–109: Corbis; p. 110: PhotoDisc, Inc.; p. 113: PhotoDisc, Inc.; p. 115: PhotoDisc, Inc.; p. 116: PhotoDisc, Inc.; p. 117: Comstock; p. 118: PhotoDisc, Inc.; p. 119: PhotoDisc, Inc.; p. 120: PhotoDisc, Inc.; p. 121: PhotoDisc, Inc.; p. 122: PhotoDisc, Inc.

 For more writing practice: www.timeforkids.com/hh/writeideas

Table of Contents

Using Your Writer's Notebook **4**

Section 1: Words **5**

Grammar and Usage • Choosing Words Wisely • Nouns • Verbs • Pronouns • Adjectives • Adverbs • Conjunctions • Prepositions • Commonly Misused Words • Spelling and Mechanics

Section 2: Sentences **25**

Kinds of Sentences • Sentence Parts • Sentence Structures • Run-on Sentences • Sentence Fragments • Parallel Structure • Vary Your Sentences • Punctuation

Section 3: Paragraphs **43**

Lead Paragraphs • Body Paragraphs • Conclusions

Section 4: Essays, Letters, and Résumés **53**

Common Forms of Student Writing • Narrative Essay • Literature Response Essay • Expository Essay • Persuasive Essay • College Entry Essay • Letters • Résumés

Section 5: Putting It Together: The Writing Process **93**

The Writing Process • Before You Write • Prewriting • Drafting • Revising • Editing and Proofreading • Publishing • After You Write

Index **124**

Traits of Good Writing Index **128**

Using Your Writer's Notebook

Are you a good decision-maker? As a student writer, you face many important decisions every time you put pen to paper or fingers to a keyboard. What should you write about? To whom are you writing? How do you make the text say exactly what you want it to say? And perhaps the most important decision of all—when you get stuck, to whom should you turn for advice?

The writers and editors at TIME Magazine face these same questions every day. And they know how important it is to have an easy-to-use resource that provides no-nonsense answers to writing questions the moment they arise. Your Writer's Notebook is just such a resource.

Your TIME Writer's Notebook features:

- tabbed sections that organize information using common writing terms.
- clear explanations and examples of writing rules and concepts, including complete examples of common student writing forms.
- special materials for generating ideas at the beginning of the writing process and for troubleshooting problems along the way.
- pointed writing strategies and tips from TIME editors.

Think of your Writer's Notebook as a trusted writing partner. Follow its outline of the writing process to make writing tasks more manageable. Use its example essays as models for your own work. Keep the book close by to find quick answers to tricky questions of grammar and punctuation. When you make this notebook your writing partner, you increase your chances of writing success.

Words

You communicate with others in many ways. As a baby, you used cries to express happiness or discomfort. Later, you learned your first word, and then more words, until you could use language to communicate a wide range of emotions and ideas. Then and now, words are the building blocks of your language skills. This section of your Writer's Notebook explains how to identify and choose accurate, stylish words for many student writing situations.

Grammar and Usage

Words in all languages follow rules. These rules are not meant to restrict your freedom as a writer (there are reasons why you may want to break the rules sometimes). Rather, language rules help writers and readers develop a common understanding of what texts really mean. Without these rules, communication breaks down.

Grammar rules identify the role a word plays in a sentence. For example, all words have names—such as *noun, verb,* and *adjective*—that identify their patterns of use. Note the red words below:

He crawled through a **hatch** in the floor and disappeared.
The eggs **hatched** after 28 days.

In the first sentence, *hatch* is a noun and refers to a small door. *Hatched,* however, is a past tense verb that describes a baby bird emerging from its shell. Knowing parts of speech and other grammar rules will help you use such words accurately and effectively.

Usage is the way people actually use a word to express themselves. Usage and grammar work together to help you decide which word should be used in a specific situation. These rules are especially helpful when you must choose between two words that look or sound alike, as below:

The cause of the problem is clear, but its **effect** is yet to be seen.
How did your performance on the exam **affect** your final grade?

The red words are easily confused. However, if they are removed, grammar rules state that the first sentence will need a noun and the second sentence a verb. If you also know the usage for *effect* (a noun meaning "a result") and *affect* (a verb meaning "to influence"), then you can confidently choose the correct word for each sentence.

TIME Editors' Tip

Many students are afraid of the number and complexity of grammar rules and usage situations. However, there is an easy way to overcome this fear. Read! Like a musician who listens to a wide range of music, reading widely and often will help you tune your "internal ear" to how language works—and how it doesn't.

Choosing Words Wisely

Knowing grammar and usage is just the beginning of learning to use words more effectively. You should also know how the words you choose affect what you are trying to say and how you say it. Notice how different words affect the **meaning** of the sentences below:

> When Carlos walked in the door, the **giggling** started.

> When Carlos walked in the door, the **snickering** started.

Giggling, or laughing lightly, has a lighthearted, positive meaning, while *snickering* is sly giggling and has a negative meaning. In the first sentence, then, Carlos is the object of friendly amusement, while in the second sentence he is the object of ridicule.

Also, notice how different words change the **intensity** of these sentences:

> Janet was worried. She **opened** the door and **went** inside.

> Janet was worried. She **threw** open the door and **raced** inside.

The first sentence is matter-of-fact, and the reader understands perfectly the actions expressed. However, the words in the second sentence create a vivid picture of the actions in the reader's mind. The second sentence is much more dynamic and interesting to read.

Finally, word choice helps make your writing *yours;* it is part of your **style,** or the unique way you use language to express yourself. Whether you want to appear serious or funny, subtle or bold, paying careful attention to word choice will help you develop your own personal writing style.

Think Again

Sometimes writers give readers too much of a good thing. **Wordiness** is using many words to make a point that could be made just as well—and often better—with fewer words. Here are some examples of wordiness you should avoid:

Redundancy: You can tell a lot about people by their **clothes** that they wear.

Too many modifiers: He plays the piano **elegantly,** suavely, and smoothly.

Unnecessary words: At this in point in time **Now** we should try something else.

Nouns

Teacher, library, computer, concentration— how could you possibly describe a typical day at school without nouns? A **noun** is a word that names a person, place, object, or idea.

Kinds of Nouns

Writers use different kinds of nouns to identify and draw attention to the world around them.

A **common noun** names a general person, place, object, or idea. Common nouns are not capitalized unless they start a sentence.

Person	student, teacher
Place	school, nation
Object	computer, boat
Idea	language, religion

Go ahead, call me common!

A **proper noun** names a specific person, place, object, or idea. Proper nouns are always capitalized.

Person	Carla Garcia, Mr. Thomson
Place	Hamilton Middle School, United States
Object	Univac, *Titanic*
Idea	English, Christianity

A **collective noun** names a group.

team	chorus	quartet	committee

By choosing nouns carefully, you can direct your readers to notice things they previously overlooked, or to think about common objects in new ways. Notice how different nouns affect the meaning of these sentences:

> This is the **door** to the **classroom**.

> This is the **gateway** to a better **education**.

The first sentence simply names an object. The second sentence, however, uses nouns symbolically to create a very different meaning. The noun *gateway* identifies an entrance that is much more open and welcoming than the flat face of a door. And while *classroom* names a specific place, the noun *education* usually has a number of associated meanings, such as personal growth and increased opportunity.

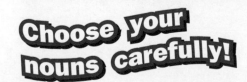
Choose your nouns carefully!

Noun Cases

Noun cases tell how a noun is related to other words in a sentence. There are three noun cases.

A **subject case** noun performs or takes the main action in a sentence or phrase. Subject nouns usually occur before the verb.

> Our **teacher** clearly **said**, "Your **homework is** due tomorrow."

> **Meredith** and her **sister left** softball practice early.

An **object case** noun receives the action in a sentence or is the object of a preposition. Object nouns are usually found after the verb, but not always.

> I **went home** for **lunch**.

> **On** sunny **days**, Mr. Winchell often **holds class** outside.

A **possessive case** noun shows ownership. Possessive nouns may occur anywhere in a sentence, but they are always found near the noun or noun phrase that is owned.

> **Miguel's computer** is not working today.

> I cringed as I listened to the story of **Lita's** recent **failure**.

Definitely a possessive case!

Think Again

Some nouns actually identify actions, but in a unique way. A **gerund** is a noun made by adding *-ing* to a verb. The gerund can then occur in any of the usual noun cases:

adding -ing to a verb

Subject: **Talking** won't get you anywhere; only **doing** will.
Object: Our music teacher appreciates my **singing**.
Possessive: Your **writing's** tone is good, but the grammar needs work.

Despite grumbles from some writers and editors, gerunds are becoming increasingly popular, especially in business and technical writing. Gerunds such as *branding, downloading,* and *outsourcing* are now widely used by writers in general. Be careful not to overuse such gerunds, though; they can make your writing overly technical and difficult to understand.

Verbs

A **verb** is word that names an action or a state of being. Verbs and verb phrases are often the most complicated part of sentences. They set your writing in motion, and doing so requires a lot of equipment, such as suffixes, helping words, and irregular forms.

Common Verb Forms and Tenses

The **infinitive form** takes the word *to* and the base form of the verb. Infinitive tense verbs can occur alone or with other verbs.

To get to school on time, I wake up at 5:30 A.M.
I went **to see** the football team play last week in the new stadium.

A **tense** is a verb form that expresses when an action or state of being occurred. You can form different tenses by changing the verb's spelling, adding a suffix, or using a helping verb.

The **present tense** indicates an action that is happening at the time of writing or an action that happens regularly. To form the present tense, use the base form of the verb or add -*s* or -*es*.

I **understand** what you are saying.
The train **passes** our house every day at noon.

The **present perfect tense** shows a completed action or an action that began in the past and continues in the present. To form the present perfect tense, use the present tense of the verb *to have* and the past participle of the main verb.

I **have done** my homework.
Our class **has studied** hard all semester.

TIME Editors' Tip

A **participle** is a verb form that is used to create the present perfect and past perfect tenses. Present participles end in -*ing*. Past participles usually end in -*ed*, but some words have irregular forms.

Present participle
walking
loving
eating
dealing
seeing

Past participle
walked
loved
eaten
dealt
seen

The **past tense** indicates an action that took place before the writing. To form the past tense of regular verbs, add the suffix *-d* or *-ed* to the base form of the verb. Irregular verbs take spelling changes in the past tense instead of a suffix.

Yesterday we **played** outside in the rain.
We **ran** inside when it **started** to thunder.

The **past perfect tense** shows a past action that happened before another past action. To form the past perfect tense, use *had* and the past participle of the main verb.

We **had finished** the exam by the time the teacher **told** us to put down our pencils.
I **had** never **seen** that man before I **ran** into him today in the store.

The **future tense** indicates an action that will happen in the future. The future tense is formed using *will* or *shall* and the base form of the main verb.

For our next class trip, we **will visit** the aquarium.
When **shall** I **take** down the posters?

Subject-Verb Agreement

In most sentences, the subject(s) and verb(s) must agree in number. Singular subjects take singular verbs, and plural subjects take plural verbs.

Singular subject	This **computer crashes** every time I use it.
Combined subject	**Juan and Sharon plan** to attend college this fall.
Plural subject	Newer **cars have** excellent safety features.

Collective nouns name more than one of something, but they take singular verbs.

The **band plays** in the theater this afternoon.

However, proper collective nouns, such as band names or sports teams, usually take a verb that agrees in number.

The **Rolling Stones are** my favorite band.
U2 is playing a sold-out show tonight.

We are gathered here...

"Stay active!"

Active Voice and Passive Voice

When you speak, you use your voice to pass on information to others. By changing the tone or volume of your voice, you can draw attention to particular actions or ideas. Verbs also express actions with a particular "voice." **Voice** is the form a verb takes to show whether the subject of a sentence performs the action or receives the action. Writers use two verb voices to emphasize different information in a sentence.

In the **active voice,** the subject performs the action. Note how use of the active voice in the sentences below draws attention to the action itself and the people doing the action:

Katie and **Xuan inspected** the test tube carefully.
We wash the dishes every evening.

In the **passive voice,** the subject receives the action. Passive voice verbs are formed using the appropriate tense of the verb *to be* and the past participle of the main verb. Note how use of the passive voice in the following sentences focuses attention on the object that receives the action, rather than the action itself:

The **test tube was inspected** carefully by both scientists.
The **dishes are washed** every evening.

TIME Editors' Tip

The active voice is considered the stronger verb form. Unless there is a specific reason not to—for example, you don't know who or what does the action or you want to vary your sentence structure—try to use the active voice whenever possible in your writing.

Pronouns

A **pronoun** is a word that takes the place of a noun. Writers use pronouns to replace words that would otherwise be used over and over again in a sentence or paragraph.

As with nouns, pronouns have three cases.

Subject case	I, he, she, it, we, you, they, who, whoever
Object case	me, him, her, it, us, you, them, whom, whomever
Possessive case	mine, his, hers, its, ours, yours, theirs, whose

A pronoun usually has an **antecedent,** which is a word that occurs earlier in the text and which the pronoun replaces. A pronoun must agree in number (plural or singular) and gender (male, female, or neutral) with the word it replaces. Notice how pronouns from each case replace antecedents in the second paragraph below. Which paragraph is easier to read?

Mr. Burton is a great teacher. Sometimes, Mr. Burton brings in Mr. Burton's guitar and plays the guitar for the class. Mr. Burton teaches the class songs, and the class and Mr. Burton all sing together.

Mr. Burton is a great teacher. Sometimes, **he** brings in **his guitar** and plays **it** for the **class. He** teaches **us** songs, and **we** all sing together.

Think Again

Which is correct—*Jennifer and I* or *Jennifer and me*? When you talk to friends, it sounds more natural to say *Jennifer and me*. When you talk to a teacher, though, you may think it is more polite to say *Jennifer and I*. But watch out! When a phrase like *Jennifer and I* is the subject of a sentence, *I* is the correct pronoun. If the phrase is the object of a sentence, the correct pronoun is *me*.

Jennifer and I went to the store for my mother.

My mother sent **Jennifer and me** to the store.

You and me or you and I? That is the question!

Kind of Pronouns

Use the information below to help you identify and choose the right pronoun for your writing situation.

Personal pronouns stand for a person or thing. They are the most commonly used pronouns. The pronouns listed on page 13 are all personal pronouns.

> When the **puppy** became excited, **it** chased **its** tail for several minutes.

> Miss Stanton asked the **students** to remember **their** homework.

Compound personal pronouns end with *-self* or *-selves*. They include *myself, yourself, himself, herself, itself, ourselves, yourselves,* and *themselves*. These prounouns are used to rename the subject of a sentence or to emphasize another noun or pronoun.

> **Andy** cooked dinner for **himself.**

> **I myself** would never do such a thing.

Relative pronouns introduce adjective or noun clauses in a sentence. *Who, whom, whose, that, which, what, whose, whatever, whoever, whomever,* and *whichever* are all relative pronouns.

> The man **who** owns the shop has **what** I want.

Indefinite pronouns do not stand in for a particular person or thing. Indefinite pronouns include *another, any, each, few, many, all, some, nothing, none, one, everyone,* and *everything*.

> **One** who has lost **everything** has **nothing** left to lose.

TIME Editors' Tip

Writers once used *he* whenever the gender of an antecedent was unknown. Today, most people prefer the phrases *he or she* and *his or her*. Watch out, though! Do not substitute the plural forms *them* and *their* for these singular pronouns. If you want to use a plural pronoun, rewrite the sentence.

> Each **writer** is responsible for the quality of **his or her** own work.

> All **writers** are responsible for the quality of **their** work.

Adjectives

An **adjective** is a word that describes a noun, pronoun, or other adjective. An adjective answers the questions *which one? what kind?* or *how many?* Most adjectives come before the noun or pronoun they describe:

They live in **the big**, **dark-blue house** on Chestnut Hill.
My brother just bought **an old used car** to fix up and drive around.

When you use more than one adjective, be sure to put them in the right order.

Example 1	We found **two fun, red metal baking pans**.
Example 2	**The large, old, round, French clock** still keeps time accurately.

	Example 1	Example 2
Article		The
Number	two	
Opinion	fun	
Size		large
Age		old
Shape		round
Color	red	
Origin		French
Material	metal	
Purpose	baking	

Most adjectives have **comparative** and **superlative** forms. To form the comparative, add *-er* or *-ier* to most one and two-syllable words. Longer words take the word *more* plus the adjective. To form the superlative, add *-est, -iest* or *most* plus the adjective. Some adjectives are irregular and have to be remembered.

Adjective	Comparative	Superl.
big	bigger	biggest
busy	busier	busiest
good	better	best
bad	worse	worst

TIME Editors' Tip

When an adjective is made from a capitalized proper noun, the adjective is also capitalized.

America — American

Paris — Parisian

which one? what kind? or how many?

Adverbs

An **adverb** is a word that describes a verb, an adjective, another adverb, or even an entire sentence. An adverb answers the questions *how? when? where?* or *to what degree?* Many adverbs are formed by adding the suffix *-ly* to an adjective. Other adverbs have no other form.

quick — **quickly**	slow — **slowly**
very so now here	

An adverb usually occurs just before or after the verb, adverb, or adjective it modifies. Some adverbs stand alone at the beginning of a sentence.

We crept **nervously** up the stairs and rang the bell.	The television played **very loudly** in the empty room.	**Luckily**, my brother returned **promptly** last night.

In general, rules for forming **comparative** and **superlative** forms of adverbs are the same as for adjectives. To form the comparative, add *-er* or *-ier* to the shorter words. Longer words take the word *more* plus the adverb. To form the superlative, add *-est, -iest* or *most,* plus the adverb.

Adverb	soon easily quickly little well
Comparative form	sooner easier more quickly less better
Superlative form	soonest easiest most quickly least best

Conjunctions

A **conjunction** is a word that connects words, phrases, clauses, or sentences. If you use conjunctions properly, your writing will flow easily from one idea to the next. *And, or, but, for, so,* and *yet* are the most commonly used conjunctions.

I like meat **and** vegetables, **but** I don't like to eat them together.
Would you like milk **or** water?

Some conjunctions are used in pairs, such as *either/or, neither/nor, both/and, just as/so, not only/but also,* and *whether/or.*

Neither Thom **nor** Rosa like where they live.
Not only is it loud, **but** there is **also** no place to sit down.

Prepositions

A **preposition** is a word that relates nouns and pronouns to other words and parts of a sentence. Proper use of prepositions helps your readers understand the following information:

Time	meet **at** ten o'clock	leave **in** five minutes
Place	the book **in** the library	wait **at** her desk
Direction	run **toward** the station	drive **around** the block
Association	go **with** your friend	the top **of** the mountain
Purpose	money **for** milk	the key **to** success

Prepositions often occur in idiomatic phrases. This means that the phrase's meaning is unrelated to the individual words that make up the phrase, as in "**on top of [taking care of]** the problem" and "**beside** herself **[very upset]** with worry."

Commonly Misused Words

Below is a list of words and phrases that writers often use incorrectly. Consult this list when you have difficulty choosing between words that have similar spellings, pronunciations, or meanings.

a, an	Use *a* before words that begin with consonants and *an* before words that begin with vowels or vowel sounds. **a** car **an** apple **a** 400-meter race **an** hour

affect, effect	*Affect* is usually a verb meaning "to influence"; *effect* is a noun meaning "result," or a verb meaning "to bring about" or "to result in."
	
	    Smoking can negatively **affect** your health
	
	    Cancer and emphysema are two **effects** of smoking.
	
	    All her research **effected** a cure for the disease.

can, may	*Can* means an action is possible; *may* means an action is allowed.
	
	    Practice has been cancelled, so I **can** go home now.
	
	    You **may** leave the table when you are finished.

farther, further	*Farther* refers to distance; *further* usually means "more."
	
	    I traveled **farther** than five miles on my bike.
	
	    Further studies are needed to know for sure.

have, of	The words *could, must, should,* and *would* should never be followed by *of*; use *have* only.
	
	    I **should ~~of~~ have** taken more time to revise my paper.
	
	    We **would ~~of~~ have** gone to the game if it hadn't rained.

its, it's	*Its* is a possessive pronoun; *it's* is a contraction of *it* and *is*.
	
	    The dog was chasing **its** tail.
	
	    It's no secret that Eli plans to go to college.

than, then	*Than* is a conjunction used for comparison; *then* is an adverb indicating time.
	
	    My sister is older **than** I am.
	
	    Eat your dinner and **then** you may have dessert.

their, they're, there	*Their* is a possessive pronoun; *they're* is the contraction of *they* and *are*; *there* is an adverb. That is **their** new house. **They're** very excited about it. They lived **there** briefly.
title, entitle	*Title* and *entitle* both mean "to name"; *entitle* also means "to have a claim to something." I **titled** the song "For Emily." This ticket **entitles** you to free admission.
to, too, two	*To* is a preposition of direction; *too* is an adverb meaning "also"; *two* is a number. I am going **to** the movies. Will you and Sara come, **too**? I have **two** extra tickets.
weather, whether	*Weather* refers to the state of the atmosphere; *whether* is a conjunction used to introduce an alternative. Is the **weather** stormy today? It depends on **whether** or not the hurricane hits land.
who's, whose	*Who's* is a contraction of *who* and *is*; *whose* indicates possession. **Who's** coming with us tonight? **Whose** coat is this?
your, you're	*Your* is a possessive pronoun; *you're* is a contraction of *you* and *are*. Listen to **your** parents. **You're** the leader now.

TIME Editors' Tip

When you are unsure whether to use a contraction or its pronoun homophone (a word that sounds like another word), simply read the sentence using the two base words of the contraction. If the two words make sense in the sentence, then the contraction is the correct word. If they do not, use the pronoun.

Where is **their** car parked?

It's (it is) its a matter of national importance.

Spelling and Mechanics

The previous pages in this section of your Writer's Notebook outline how words work and how to choose them wisely. However, there is still another question about words that many writers find difficult to answer: *How should my words actually look on the page?* If you are unable to answer this question successfully, readers may find your text confusing or receive a very different meaning than the one you intended.

Spelling words correctly is one way to make sure that readers understand exactly what you are trying to say. Keep in mind that the spelling of English words has developed over many years and continues to develop today. In fact, there is no single authority on how certain sounds should be spelled—even dictionaries can disagree! Still, notice how a single letter dramatically changes the meaning of the sentences below:

| Go **forth**. — Go **fourth**. |
| I am **dyeing**. — I am **dying**. |

Mechanics refers to how words look on the page, but this issue is about more than just appearances. The typeface you use or the decision to spell out a number or symbol can greatly affect the audience's experience and understanding of your text. Note how mechanics changes the meaning and readability of the sentences below:

| dr. chow's 2 favorite movies are gone with the wind and lost in space. |
| Dr. Chow's two favorite movies are *Gone with the Wind* and *Lost in Space*. |

In the second sentence, changing the numeral to the word *two* is much easier on the reader's eyes. But more importantly, without proper mechanics the first sentence means that Dr. Chow's favorite movies cannot be found. Use mechanical rules for capital letters, italics, and numbers to tell your readers exactly what you want them to know— the titles of Dr. Chow's two favorite movies.

Commonly Misspelled Words

Does *acceptable* end with *-ible* or *-able*? Is there one *r* and *s* in *embarrassment*, or two? It is a common complaint among writers that English contains many words that are difficult to spell. The following list contains some of the most frequently misspelled words:

acceptable	neighbor
accommodate	noticeable
acquire	occasionally
embarrass(ment)	occurrence
a lot	pastime
argument	principal/principle
calendar	pronunciation
category	receipt
collectible	receive
column	recommend
definite(ly)	rhyme
experience	rhythm
height	schedule
independent	separate
its/it's	their/they're/there
kernel/colonel	twelfth
library	until
license	weather/whether
lightning	weird
misspell	

TIME Editors' Tip

There are many ways to catch spelling mistakes in your writing. One way is to remember a few reliable spelling rules. Little songs or rhymes, such as the following, can help you remember these rules: "Use *i* before e, except after *c,* or when pronounced *ay,* as in *neighbor* or *weigh*."

> *i* **before** *e:*
> belief, chief, niece, friend

> *ei* **after** *c:*
> ceiling, deceit, receive

> *ei* **pronounced** *ay:*
> weigh, freight, eight

The spell check feature in most word processing software also will help you catch many spelling mistakes. However, it won't catch words that are spelled correctly but used incorrectly, such as using *to* when you want to say *too*, or words that are misspelled to form another word, such as *form* instead of *from*. Of course, a dictionary is always a helpful spelling tool. Say the word aloud and listen for its initial sound to pinpoint where you are likely to find the word in the dictionary.

Capital Letters

To **capitalize** a word, write the first letter in the word as an uppercase, or capital, letter. There are a number of rules for capitalization in English.

Always capitalize the first word of a sentence, including a sentence of quoted speech or dialogue.

My father always tells me, "**D**o as I say, not as I do."

Always capitalize proper nouns and adjectives.

Martin **L**uther **K**ing, **J**r.
Victorian architecture
the **B**ronx **Z**oo

Always capitalize the important words in media titles (books, songs, movies, and so on).

Harry Potter and the Goblet of Fire
"**W**hen **S**eptember **E**nds"

Always capitalize the names of businesses, organizations, and other institutions.

U.S. Congress
Standard **E**ngineering **C**ompany
the **U**niversity of **F**lorida

Capitalize the individual letters in acronyms, or words formed from the initial letters of other words, when the words forming the acronym are capitalized.

U.S.A. (**U**nited **S**tates of **A**merica)
DMV (**D**epartment of **M**otor **V**ehicles)

Capitalize abbreviated titles before and after a name.

Dr. Karen Mulder, **M.D.**
Mr. Nelson William Page, **S**r.

Italics

Italics are letters that slant to the right. Using italics draws attention to words or sets them apart from other words in the sentence. They should only be used in certain situations.

Italics are used for a variety of **names and titles.** (You may choose to underline names and titles instead of using italics, although it's not as elegant.)

Books	*Charlotte's Web*
Newspapers	*San Jose Mercury News*
Magazines, journals	*National Geographic*
Online magazines, journals	*TIME.com*
Web sites, home pages	*yahoo.com*
Long poems	*The Wasteland*
Plays	*Death of a Salesman*
Long musical works	*The Phantom of the Opera*
Movies	*Just Like Heaven*
Television programs	*Survivor*
Ships, trains, and aircraft	*Titanic, Orient Express, Challenger*

Italics are also used to place **emphasis** on certain words in a text.

"I *told* you it was broken!" exclaimed Nikki.

I have never seen a coyote, but I *have* heard one.

Words and phrases used as specific terms usually take italics.

How is *repetitious* spelled, anyway?

The phrase *freedom of speech* means different things to different people.

Finally, italics are used for **foreign words** in English text.

"*Gracias!*" the woman yelled excitedly.

He has a certain *je ne sais quoi* about him.

Names of sacred books, such as the Bible or the Koran, are neither italicized nor put in quotation marks; they are simply capitalized.

Scripture says…

Numbers

There are several different ways to handle numbers in written text. Sometimes you can use a numeral, or figure, such as 125; other times, you must spell out the word. Generally, it is recommended that you spell out a number if you can do so in one or two words.

The English alphabet has **twenty-six** letters.
There are only **two** pancakes in a short stack of pancakes.
We obtained **4,327** signatures on our petition.

When there are several numbers in a sentence, they all should be treated the same way, except when confusion may occur.

In the past **10** years, our soccer team has won **112** games and lost only **6**.
Bring me **two** **3**-foot boards and **ten** **2**-inch nails.

Following is a brief list of other situations that require numerals:

Addresses	**150** Pine St. Manchester, NH **03103**
Dates	February **16, 1947** May **2005**
Exact times	**10** A.M. **10:14** P.M.
Percentages and fractions	**95**% **4.82**% **7/16**
Sums of money	$**4** million £**6.9** billion
Measurements	**100** meters **16** pounds **72**˚F
Page numbers	Turn to page **3**. Pages **35** and **40** are finished.

TIME Editors' Tip

Never begin a sentence with a numeral. Instead, rewrite the sentence to move the numeral deeper into the text.

874 students currently attend Lincoln High School.

Lincoln High School currently enrolls **874** students.

Sentences

"Here's my report card, Mom." "You're out!" "We can't afford it." We use sentences to convey some of our most important ideas. A sentence is a group of words that express a complete thought. Sentences can explain, describe, inquire, command, persuade, or motivate. This section of your Writer's Notebook identifies common kinds of sentences and sentence parts. It also explains how to fix common mistakes and change the structure of your sentences to add interest to a text. Finally, this section explains the role punctuation marks play in producing accurate, expressive sentences.

Kinds of Sentences

Scan a few pages of this text. What sentence endings do you see? Punctuations marks such as periods, question marks, and exclamation points are clues that point to the different kinds of sentences. Each kind of sentence expresses a different idea or emotion.

Statements are the most common sentences. Writers use statements to describe, explain, observe, or narrate. Statements end with a period.

My book report is due tomorrow.
Rhonda believes that vegetarianism is a natural, healthy way to eat.

Commands tell someone what to do. In some commands, the person or persons being spoken to are named. In commands that do not name a specific person, the implied subject is *you*.

Commands can end with a period or an exclamation point.

Rita, hand me that screwdriver by the toolbox.
Get out of here before I lose my temper!

Exclamations convey sorrow, surprise, or other outbursts of feeling. They always end with an exclamation point.

Congratulations on your new job!
I don't know what that thing is, but it's coming this way!

Questions ask a reader or listener for information. They always end with a question mark.

How did Kelly learn how to fix computers?
If I gave you some money, would you get me a sandwich?

TIME Editors' Tip

In 2005, the American Film Institute published a list of the top 100 movie quotes of all time. What kind of sentence is each movie quote below? How does the kind of sentence affect each quote's idea or emotion?

"I'm the king of the world!"   **"Go ahead. Make my day."**
"There's no place like home."   **"Who's on first?"**

Action!

Sentence Parts

Sentences contain different parts that work together to express your ideas. Learn to identify the sentence parts below to build strong, varied sentences.

Every complete sentence must contain a subject and a predicate. The **subject** is the person, idea, or thing that a sentence is about. It can be a noun, a group of nouns, or a noun phrase. In a command, the subject is often an implied *you*. The **predicate** contains the verb or verbs that describe the action or state of being of the subject. Some predicates are single words and others contain groups of words.

Subject	Predicate
Puppies	**bark.**
The local **newspaper**	**sent** a reporter to the game.
Julio and **I**	**watched** the game and **ate** popcorn.
[You]	**Pick** up that pencil.

A **clause** is a group of words that contains a subject and a verb. An independent clause can stand alone as a sentence. A dependent clause does not make sense if it stands alone. A dependent clause is usually introduced by an adverb, adjective, or other word.

Independent clauses	**We argued for hours**, but **we could not agree**.
Dependent clause	The things **that you believe to be true** arc not necessarily facts.

A **phrase** is a group of words that serves the purpose of a noun, adverb, or adjective. Like nouns, some phrases serve as the subject of a sentence. Like adjectives and adverbs, phrases can also describe other words.

Subject phrases	**Doing your homework** every night is a good habit. **To err** is human, **to forgive** is divine.
Descriptive phrases	The **dog with the big ears** is mine. **Slowing briefly**, the **runner** drank some water.

Sentence Structures

The **structure** of a sentence depends on the number and relationship of its parts.

A **simple sentence** contains a simple subject and a simple predicate.

> **We [sub.] visited [pred.]** Colorado.

A **simple sentence with a compound subject** contains two or more subjects and one predicate.

> My **sister [sub.] and I [sub.] built [pred.]** a fire.

A **simple sentence with a compound predicate** contains one subject and two or more predicates.

> **We [sub.] hiked [pred.]** in the hills and **camped [pred.]** next to a stream.

A **compound sentence** contains two independent clauses.

> **I [sub.] slept [pred.]** in a tent, and my **sister [sub.] slept [pred.]** in a hammock.

A **complex sentence** contains one independent clause and one or more dependent clauses.

> **We [sub.] slept [pred.]** in a tent **that we bought for the trip [dep. clause].**

A **compound-complex sentence** contains two or more independent clauses and at least one dependent clause.

> The **fines [sub.] that you pay on library books [dep. clause] increase [pred.]** daily, so **you [sub.] should return [pred.]** them promptly.

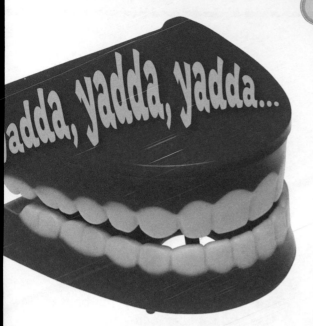

yadda, yadda, yadda...

Run-on Sentences

Everybody knows someone who jabbers on and on without pausing or hesitating when moving from one point to the next one. The same behavior takes place in writing. **Run-ons** are sentences that go on far too long, forcing the reader to plow through line after line of confusing text. There are two common causes of run-ons:

Merged sentences with no punctuation. A common error is to run phrases and clauses together with no punctuation marks to separate the thoughts, as in the examples below.

Our state grows corn a seed crop as well as a food crop and other agricultural products.
What I want is for us to help poor people I feel so sad when I see them on television.

Sentences are merged with too many commas. It's also confusing to string phrases along with commas, not indicating any order of importance:

I couldn't sleep because it was too dark, and I was cold, plus my sister talked all night and she snored when she fell asleep, and the ground was hard.

Fixing Run-ons

Use the techniques below to turn run-ons into balanced, readable sentences.

Fix: Add a connecting word.
Run-on: We stayed up late we were watching the stars.
Fixed: We stayed up late **because** we were watching the stars.

Fix: Add punctuation.
Run-on: The veto is how the president the executive branch says no to a new law.
Fixed: The veto is how the president (the executive branch) says no to a new law.

Fix: Create two or more sentences.
Run-on: What I want is for us see poor people I feel so sad them on television. us to help ad whe
Fixed: What I poor peop them

30

Sen

Sentence Fragments

A **fragment** is an incomplete sentence. It may start with a capital letter and have proper punctuation, but a fragment lacks a subject, a predicate, or both.

Fixing Fragments

Use these techniques to turn fragments into strong, complete sentences.

Fix: Add a noun or noun phrase.
Fragment: In Kentucky was born.
Fixed: Abraham Lincoln was born in Kentucky.

Fix: Add a verb or verb phrase.
Fragment: Later, Lincoln ending slavery.
Fixed: Later, Lincoln **debated** ending slavery.

Fix: Add a subject and a verb.
Fragment: Honest Abe, Father Abraham, and the Great Emancipator.
Fixed: People [subject] called [verb] him Honest Abe, Father Abraham, and the Great Emancipator.

Fix: Cut a connecting word.
Fragment: Because they thought he was a wise and capable leader.
Fixed: [Because] **T**hey thought he was a wise and capable leader.

FRAGMENTS BUILD MOOD!
Split-second scene described!

Think Again

You should avoid sentence fragments in most writing situations, but sometimes fragments can help you express your ideas in unusual and interesting ways. In fiction and in sports reporting, for example, fragments can build moods or describe split-second action.

Mood: Drenching rain. Lightning. A falling tree. Crash! And then nothing more, until now, in this hospital bed.

A he quarterback pauses. Looking for an opening. Can't find it. hes down. Charges through. Flat on his back now, but over line. And now a champion, at last.

entences

Parallel Structure

In grammar, **parallel structures** have the same or similar construction. For example, the verbs *talked* and *ran* are parallel, because both verbs are in the past tense. The verbs *talked* and *are running* are not parallel, however, because they are in different tenses. Parallelism makes sentences more elegant and effective, as in the examples below.

Type of construction	Not parallel	Parallel
Multiple predicates	I **played** video games and **was watching** TV.	I **played** video games and **watched** TV.
Nouns in a series	Good sentences depend on **punctuation, word choice,** and **varying the structure.**	Good sentences depend on **punctuation**, **word choice**, and **variety of structure**.
One modifier referring to a series of nouns	For school I have **new** jeans, sweaters, and **bigger** shoes.	For school I have **new** jeans, sweaters, and shoes.
Phrases in a series	I sing **in** the shower, the breakfast table, and always **out of** tune.	I sing **in** the shower, **at** the breakfast table, and always **out of** tune.

TIME Editors' Tip

Use parallel structure to write strong, memorable sentences. Consider these well-known examples from *Poor Richard's Almanac,* written by Benjamin Franklin in the 1700s. Are these ideas as memorable without parallel structure?

Not parallel	Parallel
When you **save** a **penny**, it is like you **earned** that **money**.	**A penny saved** is **a penny earned**
Going to bed early and then **getting an early start** to the day will make you **feel better in many ways.**	**Early to bed** and **earl~~...~~** a man **healthy, w~~...~~**

Vary Your Sentences

Vary your sentences to give words more impact and keep the reader's interest. In the examples below, notice how changes to a sentence's length and structure cause other changes in emphasis, style, and tone.

Change the Length

Use sentences of different lengths to change your audience's reading pace and to vary the rhythm of your text. Short sentences move faster and can help you build suspense or make strong points. Long sentences give you room to add interesting details. They are also useful for creating moods, describing settings, and making lists.

Shorten sentences	Long	Shorter
Remove unnecessary adjectives and adverbs.	I'm usually sound asleep when the first light of dawn breaks.	I'm usually asleep when dawn breaks.
Remove unnecessary phrases and clauses.	As I often say, I really like pizza.	I really like pizza.
Restate phrases and clauses as single words.	My dad and mom met when they were in the same science class in college.	My parents met in a college science class.

Lengthen sentences	Short	Longer
Break a process into steps.	She made a peanut butter sandwich.	She cut a slice of bread, opened a jar of peanut butter, and made a sandwich.
descriptive details.	The trees change color in autumn.	In autumn, deciduous trees change from green to red and gold.
Add phr... ...auses.	Our team won the game.	The Fighting Tigers trailed in the first half but clawed their way to victory in the last quarter.

...entences

Change the Structure

Readers quickly lose interest in texts with boring, repetitive sentence structures. Changing the structure can shift emphasis to different words or alter the tone of the sentence. Use the strategies below to liven up your sentence structures and add interest to your writing.

Strategy: Rewrite sentences in different forms.
Original statement: We can pretend how it feels to fly.
Command: Imagine how it feels to fly.
Exclamation: Suddenly, you're flying!
Question: How would it feel to fly?

Strategy: Combine short sentences.
Original: Columbus went to sea as a young man. He sailed to many ports around the Mediterranean.
New: Columbus went to sea as a young man and sailed to many ports around the Mediterranean.

Strategy: Change the placement of clauses.
Original: Students listen to the principal when he speaks.
New: When the principal speaks, students listen.

TIME Editors' Tip

In all sentences, the subject noun and predicate verb must match, or agree: a singular subject takes the singular form of the verb, and a plural subject uses a plural verb form. Subject-verb disagreement often occurs in sentences that contain phrases or clauses. Here is a trick to help you discover whether your subjects and predicates agree. First, identify the potentially misleading phrase. Then, pretend it's not there. When this phrase disappears, you can more easily identify the sentence's actual subject and predicate and determine whether or not they agree.

The **number** [of portable stereo options] ~~increase~~ **increases** every year.

[Somewhere in this boo~~are is~~ the **answer** tomorrow's q

Punctuation

When you speak, you pause frequently to take a breath or allow the listener to respond. Similarly, when you write you use punctuation marks to help the audience pace their reading and process meaning. **Punctuation marks** are symbols that show relationships among sentences, different parts of a sentence, or even individual words and parts of words in a sentence. When you use punctuation correctly, you will create a clear, coherent text for your readers.

The Purposes of Punctuation

Punctuation marks perform several different duties in a sentence.

- **End sentences.** Periods, question marks, and exclamation points show where a sentence ends. These punctuation marks also indicate whether a sentence is a statement, command, exclamation, or question.

- **Create pauses.** Other punctuation marks indicate pauses in the text. Commas are the most common of these marks, which also include colons, semicolons, parentheses, ~~and~~ dashes. Usually pauses ~~co~~te sentence parts that may be also ~~b~~ if read together. Pauses importa~~~~ers discern the most informatio~~~~st important ~~~~ntence.

~~~~ntences

- **Show quoted material.** Quotation marks indicate the exact words of a different writer or speaker. Quotations marks can also be used to show that a word or phrase is used ironically or humorously.

- **Show deleted material.** Finally, apostrophes and ellipses indicate where letters or words have been removed from a word or sentence. These marks help shorten a text or make its style less formal.

Periods

Use periods at the end of statements and commands.

Statement	I heard that this movie is excellent.
Command	Buy me some popcorn.

Periods may also occur in abbreviations and acronyms (an abbreviation made from the first letter of each word). In an abbreviation, the period usually occurs after the final letter. In an acronym the period is usually placed after the first letter of each shortened word.

Abbreviation	After living overseas, **Dr.** Potts is glad to be back in California.
Acronym	Luis has lived in the **U.S.A.** since he was born.

Think Again

Not all abbreviations and acronyms take periods. For example, many company names, such as AT&T (American Telegraph and Telephone) and IBM (International Business Machines), do not use periods. Likewise, state postal abbreviations, such as AL (Alabama) and WV (West Virginia), do not take periods.

TIME Editors' Tip

An exclamation point is a sign that a sentence is especially important or that it expresses a strong emotion. But watch out! An exclamation point is like a shout, and no one wants to be yelled at repeatedly. Use exclamation points sparingly in formal writing.

Exclamation Points

Use an exclamation point to signal a loud or emotional sentence or word.

Oh, this movie is horrible!
Wait! You forgot your homework!

Question Marks

Use a question mark to signal a question. In most questions the verb occurs before the subject. However, regular subject-verb statements and single words can become questions, too, when a question mark is placed at the end.

Do you want to leave?
What? My mom is here? Now?

Sometimes, question mark~~s~~ ~~series~~ after parallel phrase~~book bag?~~ of related que~~n homework?~~

Di~~d~~

Sen

36

Commas

Commas are the most common punctuation marks in sentences. A comma always indicates a pause, but these pauses serve many different functions. In some cases, commas are needed to make a sentence's meaning clear. In others, commas change a sentence's tone or style.

Items in a Series: Use commas to separate a series of words or phrases that express a similar idea. Place a comma after each item in the series except the last one.

Beautiful beaches, warm weather, and lush plant life make Florida a fun vacation spot.
Its friendly people ask **who you are, where you are from,** and **what you like to do**.
Visit Florida's beaches to **swim in the surf, play in the sand, or lie in the sun**.

Place commas between a series of adjectives or adverbs when the meaning of the sentence does not change if the words are separated by *and*.

Florida's amusement parks offer **many [and] unique [and] exciting** activities.
Florida's amusement parks offer **many unique, exciting** activities.

Compound Sentences: A compound sentence contains two or more sentences connected by a conjunction, such as *and, but,* and *or*. Place a comma before the conjunction.

We moved to San Diego four years ago. I still miss my friends in Boston.
We moved to San Diego four years ago, **but** I still miss my friends in Boston.

However, do not use commas when the joined sentences are very short.

I ran. Will walked.
I ran and Will walked.

Think Again

One reason why writers have such difficulty with commas is that different texts use different rules for comma placement. This makes it difficult to learn exactly when comma is necessary and when it is optional. For example, your 's Notebook says commas should occur after all but the an The a series. However, to save space many newspapers do it co do not use a comma between the last two items. n to you, but whatever you choose to do, may confuse your readers.

entences

The final choice is yours.

Quotations: In a quotation, commas and quotation marks set off spoken or quoted words from the rest of the sentence. Where the comma is placed depends on where in the sentence the speaker is named.

Before	Molly suddenly burst out, "I have to get out of here!"
After	"There's no reason to yell," Sam calmly explained.
Both	"When we leave," she whispered, "let's go out the back door."

Beginning Phrases: Place a comma after a long or complicated phrase at the beginning of a sentence. A prepositional phrase consists of a preposition, such as *in* or *under*, plus its object. An adverbial phrase is a phrase that acts as an adverb in a sentence. A participial phrase contains the participial form of a verb.

Prepositional phrase	**With friends like you,** who needs enemies?
Adverbial phrase	**In your own words,** tell your story.
Participial phrase	**Thinking quickly,** I grabbed the envelope from his hands.

Unneeded Clauses: Some clauses can be cut from a sentence without changing the meaning. Others must remain for the sentence to make sense. Use commas to set off unnecessary clauses.

Commas needed	Henry Aaron, **who hit 755 home runs,** is a baseball legend.
No commas	He **who runs most swiftly** wins the race.
Commas needed	Our school, **which was built just last year,** has a leaking roof.
No commas	Knowing **which way is north** is an important hiking skill.

Directed Speech: Use commas to set off the name of someone who is directly spoken to.

Michael, will you grab that folder for me?
Which one, **Mr. Douglass**?
Give me the green one, **Michael,** next to your mouse pad.

Appositives: An appositive is a noun or noun phrase that explains another noun. Appositives are usually placed right after the nouns they explain. Use commas to set off an appositive.

The pope, **the head of the Roman Catholic Church,** lives in er, grades
Mr. Jones, **our bio**... our homework...

Interjections and Exclamations:

An interjection is a word that expresses an emotion or sensation, such as *well* and *ouch*. An exclamation is a strongly emotional word or phrase, such as *hey* and *hurrah*. Use commas to set off these words whenever they occur.

Hey, be sure to send that e-mail before you leave!
Well, you should have told me earlier.
I did tell you about, **oh,** four hours ago.

Answers with Yes, No, or Maybe:

Place commas after the words *yes, no,* and *maybe* when they begin sentences and answer direct or implied questions.

No, I didn't hear about the math test tomorrow. Will it be difficult?
Maybe, so we should meet after school to study.

Greetings:

Place a comma between a word or phrase of greeting, such as *hello* or *what's up*, and the person being greeted. Also, place a comma after the greeting in a personal letter.

Greetings, earthlings.
What's up, Buttercup?
Dear **Gloria and Uncle Steve,** Thank you so much for your kind birthday

Abbreviations After Names:

Place commas around abbreviations that follow a proper name, such as academic degrees, professional organizations, and *Jr.* and *Sr.*

Drew Pinsky, **M.D.,** will speak to our health class next week.
Cecile wrote her essay about Martin Luther King, **Jr.**

Locations and Addresses:

Place commas after the name of a city and a state. Also, use commas to separate the street address, city, and state and zip code.

I lived in **Madison, Wisconsin,** for many years.
The Empire State Building is located at **350 Fifth Avenue, New York, NY 10118**.

Dates and Numbers:

In dates, place a comma after the day of the month and the year. Always place a comma between two numbers that may otherwise be confused.

Juneteenth is a holiday that celebrates **June 19, 1865,** when enslaved Texans learned they were free.
Between 2000 and **2005, 357** of our former students graduated from college.

ntences

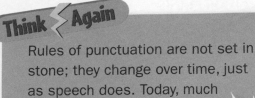
Semicolons

A semicolon works with commas to group long lists into shorter units.

> He runs, swims, or works out five hours a day; eats nothing but organically grown fruits, vegetables, and grains; and takes all kinds of vitamins.

You can also use a semicolon to separate a statement and a conclusion that can be drawn from it.

> Semicolons flourished when long sentences were in style; they became more rare when sentences grew shorter.

Colons

Use a colon before a list of items or actions.

> We've run out of these supplies: paper plates, paper cups, snacks, and soft drinks.

> Please do the following: go to the library, take out a cookbook, and bring it to me.

Colons are often used in two-part titles as well.

> *World Religions*: *An Introduction*

> "Faded Glory: Denim in America"

Think Again

Rules of punctuation are not set in stone; they change over time, just as speech does. Today, much of the information we read comes in bulleted lists. A **bullet** is a small dot or other symbol that calls attention to each item in a list. A colon often introduces the list. The bulleted items may form a complete sentence, or they may be individual phrases.

Rules of punctuation are not set in stone.

To play this game:
- insert the disk,
- select the play mode, and
- enter your initials.

Our school has many advantages:
- Small class sizes
- Sports teams
- College prep courses

Quotation Marks

Like commas, quotation marks set apart words within a sentence. Quotation marks always appear in pairs before and after a word, phrase, sentence, or group of sentences. Use quotation marks in the following situations:

A **direct quote** contains the exact words someone spoke or wrote. Direct quotes can record conversations or add an outside voice to a sentence.

"I think you and I are perfect together," he said.
As Shakespeare remarked, "All the world's a stage."

However, an indirect quote is one that is reworded by the writer. Indirect quotes *do not* take quotation marks.

Direct quote	"I will not raise taxes, no matter what happens," promised the president.
Indirect quote	The president promised he would not raise taxes under any circumstances.

Quotation marks are also used to **change the tone of a word or phrase.** The quotes signal to the reader that the writer is commenting on those words. Usually the writer's comment consists of sarcasm or irony.

The city's "improvements" included more parking lots, but no parks.

Finally, quotation marks indicate the **titles** of short works. These short works usually are part of a larger work or a collection of works, such as a book, album, television series, or magazine. (See page 23 for rules about italicizing the titles of longer works.)

Short story	"The Gift of the Magi"
Poem	"Dream Deferred"
Chapter	"The March to Yorktown"
Essay	"Bookshop Memories"
Newspaper or magazine article	"America's Best Public High Schools"
Song	"Purple Haze"
TV episode	"To Serve Man"

Quota
befor marks always appear in pairs,
after words or phrases.

sentences

Apostrophes

An **apostrophe** replaces missing letters in a word.
Contractions always contain an apostrophe.

> I **can't** make you do anything **you're** unwilling to do.

Apostrophes are also used to show possession or purpose.
This table shows how apostrophes are used to create
different kinds of possessives:

Singular noun	I like going to my **grandmother's house**.
Plural noun	The **cars' engines** started at once.
Collective noun	The book was a **children's story**.
Name that ends in s	Mrs. **Jones's dog** is smaller than the **Stevens's cat**.

Ellipses

An **ellipsis** is a series of three periods that take the place
of words that have been cut from a sentence. Use an
ellipsis to shorten a quote or to show interrupted speech.
You can also use an ellipsis at the end of a sentence to
create suspense.

Shorten a quote	We the people of the United States...do ordain and establish this Constitution for the United States of America.
Show interrupted speech	"It's just that I..." he muttered before falling silent.
Create suspense	I finally knew what had happened that night. At least, I thought I knew...

TIME Editors' Tip

Ellipses are a handy way
to cut lenghty quotes
down to size. However,
be careful when you use
ellipses that you do not
change the meaning
of the original quote.
How do the ellipses
change the meaning
of the passage below?
Is this a responsible
use of ellipses?

Original

"Congress shall make
no law respecting an
establishment of religion,
or prohibiting the free
exercise thereof; or
abridging the freedom
of speech, or of the
press; or the right of
the people peaceably to
assemble, and to petition
the Government for a
redress of grievances."

Misquote

"Congress...make...the
law...the people
aceably to assemble."

Parentheses

Parentheses surround information that, when removed, will still leave a complete sentence. Parentheses always come in pairs. Some parentheses occur within a sentence, while others occur between sentences. The text in the parentheses may be a phrase, a clause, or a complete sentence.

Like commas, parentheses may surround an appositive.

> I found my old teddy bear (the one I played with as a kid) up in the attic.

Parentheses may also contain the writer's or speaker's comments.

> Roger claims (you're not going to believe this) that he never went near the house.

One of the most important uses of parentheses is to cite sources of information.

> This idea was first developed by Albert Einstein in 1905 (Einstein 23).

You can also use parentheses to direct readers to other parts of a text.

> Some ~~by hand~~ers prefer to draft their work (See Chap than on a computer. more information.)

Dashes

A dash is a long horizontal mark that sets apart a group of words within a sentence. Dashes can take the place of commas, colons, or parentheses. Like exclamation points, they serve to emphasize ideas; therefore, they should not be overused. However, dashes are very useful for indicating sudden breaks in thought, creating suspense, or adding the punch line to a joke.

Break in thought	He promised me—not that you can believe a word he says—that I wouldn't have to go first.
Suspense	He crept up the stairs—slowly, silently, and with great fear—to investigate the strange noise.
Punch line	He's tough on the outside, soft on the inside, and often slightly cracked—in other words, he's a nut.

Parentheses and dashes set apart information in a sentence.

Paragraphs

What are your thoughts about the first day of school? Your favorite book? School uniforms? You could respond to these topics in many ways, but you probably will need to write at least one paragraph—perhaps several—to fully express your ideas. A paragraph is a group of sentences that relate to a main idea. In a longer piece of writing, each paragraph presents a distinct idea about a single topic. This section of your Writer's Notebook presents techniques for building common kinds of paragraphs. It also explains how to link separate paragraphs so that your work feels unified and whole.

Lead Paragraphs

Readers often decide if they will continue reading a work after only a few sentences, so first impressions are important. Good writers use compelling leads to draw readers into the text. A **lead** is the first paragraph in a longer work. Leads come in many forms, but a strong lead should do the following things:

- **Introduce the main idea** of the piece. In informal writing, the main idea can be implied, or stated indirectly. A formal lead contains a thesis sentence that clearly states the main point.
- **Capture the readers' attention** and make them want to read more.
- **Establish the tone** or "feel" of the piece.

Which paragraph below is the stronger lead?

> The first day of school is usually easy. Most years I just show up and get my books. Sometimes that's a lot harder than you think, though.

> I don't know why I was nervous, but I was. It certainly wasn't my first time walking into a new classroom. So why was the first day of ninth grade so much more difficult than all the first days before it?

The first lead introduces the topic, but readers are ~~by~~ to continue reading a work that begins lead ~~ng~~ complaints or excuses. The second in a way ~~s~~ up the main idea, it does so nervous ~~t~~ elate to—who hasn't been the honest ~~t~~ a new challenge? Also, author's ideas ~~s~~ believe that the

Paragraphs

Creating a Great Lead

A great lead grabs your audience's attention and draws them into your piece. Use the techniques below to launch your ideas into readers' lives.

A **compelling quote** tells readers that other persons of authority have ideas about your topic and that you recognize good writing when you see it.

> Aristotle once wrote, "It is the mark of an educated mind to be able to entertain a thought without accepting it." This mark is missing, however, in the rush to cut funding for after-school activities.

An **attention-getting statistic** shows the audience that your topic is important and worth investigating further.

> According to the American Lung Association, each day nearly 6,000 children under the age of 18 will start smoking, and nearly 2,000 of them will go on to become regular smokers. New programs seek to reduce these numbers by giving kids fun alternatives to smoking.

An **interesting example or anecdote** (personal story) can draw readers in with a compelling story or description.

> It was the final shot of the game. The basketball spun around and around the edge of the hoop until it slowed, stopped circling, and dropped into the net. Cheers rang out across the gymnasium. After four disappointing seasons, our team was finally going to the state tournament.

A **question that relates to readers' lives** shows that you have considered how your topic connects to problems or concerns that we all share.

> Have you ever said "yes" when you know you should have said "no"? When tenth-grader Justin Martin skipped Spanish class last Friday, he came to know this feeling all too well

Nice to meet you!

Think Again

Many writers prefer not to use the word *you* in their work. However, using *you* in informal pieces can make the audience feel as if they are being spoken to directly. The text becomes more personal and readers respond with greater interest.

Thesis Sentences

What's the big idea? That's the question answered by a thesis sentence. **A thesis sentence** states a formal essay's main idea or argument. A good thesis sentence should do the following things:

Provide a clear and direct statement of the main idea. In the unclear example below, the author's position on the issue appears weak and uncertain.

Unclear	If soft drink machines are banned from schools, maybe they can be replaced with juice dispensers.
Clear	Soft drink machines should be banned from schools.

Make its point fully but succinctly. Don't hide your main idea in a forest of words.

Wordy	Homework is necessary because all learning can't take place in the classroom, but an overload of homework can cause some students to become burned out.
Succinct	Homework supports classroom learning, but too much homework can lead to burnout.

Occur at the beginning of the lead paragraph or the end of the lead paragraph or the end of the

beginning of the paragraph emphasizes supporting arguments. Placement at the end of the paragraph emphasizes the main idea.

Placed at the beginning	**Parents should consult with teens when setting curfews.** Teens know their own schedules better than parents. By having some control over their schedules, teens will be more likely to adhere to a curfew.
Placed at the end	Teens know their own schedules better than parents. By having some control over their schedules, teens will be more likely to adhere to a curfew. **As a result, parents should consult with teens when setting curfews.**

Think Again

Usually, the lead paragraph contains an essay's thesis sentence. Sometimes, though, a writer withholds the clearest statement of the main idea until the end of an essay. The writer builds up evidence within the essay's body and then places the thesis sentence in the conclusion as a final "knockout punch."

Paragraphs

Body Paragraphs

The body of your essay or letter is where you really get to show the audience what you know. **Body paragraphs** provide the details, examples, and illustrations that back up the promise of information you made in the lead paragraph. All body paragraphs should follow a logical order and relate to the topic indicated in your lead.

Topic Sentences

Each body paragraph should contain a **topic sentence** that tells readers what the paragraph is about. Each topic sentence should do the following:

Clearly state a paragraph's main point. Topic sentences, like your thesis sentence, help guide your readers through the text. This path should be clear of obstacles, such as unnecessary words. Make sure that each topic sentence develops a different aspect of the thesis statement.

Thesis statement	Prom night can be a memorable but expensive affair.
Topic sentence 1	Special clothes must be bought or rented for the event.
Topic sentence 2	Dinner at a nice restaurant is usually part of the evening.
Topic sentence 3	Flowers are traditional and add to the cost of prom night.

Occur at or near the beginning of the paragraph. Such placement will prevent misunderstandings about the point of a paragraph.

> **Special clothes must be bought or rented for the event.** For example, many teen girls have to purchase their prom dresses and accessories. Teen boys, however, often choose to rent tuxedoes. Either way, the cost can be substantial.

TIME Editors' Tip

JUST SAY IT!

Some writers worry that if they clearly state each topic sentence, their essays will become boring. Therefore, they prefer to imply or hint at their main points. Too often, though, this technique only hides the main idea from the audience. When it comes to topic sentences, just say it!

Transitions

Audiences enjoy reading texts that move easily from one idea to the next. **Transitions** are words and phrases that link separate paragraphs. The following techniques will move readers smoothly through your text and make them feel that your work is unified and whole.

Repeat a key word or phrase. Echo what the audience has already read to move them smoothly on to new ideas.

Thesis sentence	Cats present a number of challenges to **pet owners**.
Paragraph 1	Among **pet owners**, cats have the reputation of being **finicky** eaters.
Paragraph 2	Cats are not only **finicky** about food, they can be very particular about their grooming as well.

Use a transitional word or phrase, such as *first, next, then, furthermore, finally, but, however, for example,* or *in addition to.* These devices help writers extend their discussion to new areas without jarring the reader.

Thesis sentence	Cats present a **number** of challenges to pet owners.
h 1	**First**, owners should be aware that cats are finicky eaters.
Paragraph	**Second**, grooming is an ~~ant~~ part of a cat's life ~~uent~~ chore for its

Paragraphs

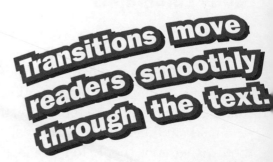

Transitions move readers smoothly through the text.

Body Builders

Use the following techniques to build a variety of strong body paragraphs.

Add details. Details take your reader further into the paragraph's main idea.

Topic sentence	There are many opportunities to exercise and have fun during winter months.
Details	Depending on where you live, the winter sporting period may begin as early as October or as late as January. Many weather services provide special forecasts for outdoor athletes during these months. Consult these forecasts to find out more about how conditions can affect your safety and performance during winter activities.

Add examples. Examples help establish your authority on a topic. Readers who already know something about your topic want to see that you have sufficient knowledge to speak to them. Less-informed readers will understand your ideas better if you provide concrete examples.

Topic sentence	There are many opportunities to exercise and have fun during winter months.
Examples	Winter sports, like skiing and snowboarding, provide fun ways to exercise outdoors. But if you prefer to stay inside, basketball is a good indoor sport. If you play basketball at a gym or fitness center, you can also take classes or wo on the weightlifting an equipment.

TIME Editors' Tip

In sports and in writing, sometimes it is necessary to make direct contact. When adding details or using examples to build body paragraphs, be sure these ideas relate to the paragraph's topic sentence and to the essay as a whole. **Digressions** are ideas that lead away from the main idea of an essay or paragraph, and they should be avoided. If the idea is truly important, put it in its own paragraph!

Paragra 50

Compare and contrast. You can present a balanced view of your topic by showing how ideas are alike or different. Always remember to compare and contrast things that relate to each other by kind (what they are) or degree (how much or how little).

Topic sentence	There are many opportunities to exercise and have fun during winter months.
Compare by kind	Downhill sports such as skiing and snowboarding require special—and often expensive—equipment. Boots, poles, skis, and snowboards must all be chosen according to your body type or snow conditions. Rentals are available on some items, but such equipment may affect your safety and performance.
Compare and contrast by degree	Favorites such as skiing and snowboarding provide a thrilling experience and stunning winter scenery. However, some people prefer less dangerous outdoor activities. Cross-country skiing is a strenuous but safe way to see snow-clad peaks and valleys. Hiking can take outdoor enthusiasts through similar areas, but at a more leisurely pace.

Show cause and effect. Identify causes and their effects to help readers analyze processes and decisions related to your topic.

Topic sentence	There are many opportunities to exercise and have fun during winter months.
...ses and ...ts	If you choose skiing as a winter sport, you will need extra money to pay for special clothing and equipment. For downhill skiing, you will also have the extra expense of lift tickets.
	Hiking is an inexpensive outdoor activity that will allow you to have extra money to save or spend on something else that you enjoy. You also will ...uce the chances of injury associated with ...ill skiing.

Paragraphs

Conclusions

You have worked hard to craft a text for your readers, so don't abandon them at the finish line. The **conclusion** is the final paragraph in an essay or letter. This paragraph provides a summary, a logical conclusion, or a final thought about your topic. The conclusion should wrap up the work in a way that is both interesting and satisfying, so that it feels complete.

Creating a Satisfying Conclusion

Many writers think that conclusions, despite their brevity, are unusually difficult to write. When these writers reach the end of the text, they may feel that they have already said everything that is worth saying or that they have simply run out of fresh ideas. However, there are several simple techniques that help writers guide audiences through to the very end of a work.

Summarize the main points. This is a very common way of concluding a work. To conclude with a summary, return to the thesis statement and present it in a new way.

Thesis statement	There are many opportunities to get exercise and have fun during winter months.
End summary	Whether you brave the outdoors or stay inside, by being open to a variety of options, you can find an exercise routine that will allow you to enjoy winter, stay fit, and have fun—all at the same time.

TIME Editors' Tip

Don't always wait to write a conclusion until you have written the lead and body paragraphs. A conclusion is a short paragraph with a defining purpose, which makes it a "miniature" version of the complete work. Drafting a conclusion early in the writing process will help you establish the thesis and tone of your work.

Return to the lead's quote, example, or anecdote. This is an especially satisfying way to conclude your work. Paired quotes are "bookends" that signal a definite beginning and end within the text. In the example below, note how the lead quote prompts readers to ask *why?* and makes them want to read on. The end quote contains a similar idea, but presents it as well-earned advice.

Lead quote	When John moved to Vermont from sunny Florida, he discovered that winter sports can be as much fun as summer sports. "Now instead of hitting the beach, I hit the slopes," he said.
End quote	John, who turned his surfboard in for a set of skis, offers this advice: "You can hit the beach, or hit the slopes. The main thing is to enjoy what you do."

Present a call to action. Some conclusions tell readers to take action as a result of what they have read. In informal writing, this call to action can be a lighthearted challenge, as in the first example below. In formal persuasive essays, the writer directs readers to respond directly to a specific proposal.

Don't let a little cold weather put a chill in your exercise routine. Get out there!
Health and fitness needs do not stop for the weather. Residents of northern states should develop a winter exercise routine that helps them stay active all year long.

End with a surprise. When introducing a new idea as a surprise ending, it should be somewhat provocative and different. Still, it must relate back to the main point in some way.

...re are a wide variety of activities availა winter ʌo people throughout the seek the ulti But for those who adventures, therⴄ winter outdoor whose members celਾolar Bear Club, Day by taking a dip in a⸗ ⴽw Year's

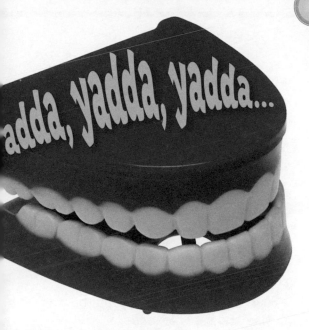

adda, yadda, yadda...

Run-on Sentences

Everybody knows someone who jabbers on and on without pausing or hesitating when moving from one point to the next one. The same behavior takes place in writing. **Run-ons** are sentences that go on far too long, forcing the reader to plow through line after line of confusing text. There are two common causes of run-ons:

Merged sentences with no punctuation. A common error is to run phrases and clauses together with no punctuation marks to separate the thoughts, as in the examples below.

> Our state grows corn a seed crop as well as a food crop and other agricultural products.

> What I want is for us to help poor people I feel so sad when I see them on television.

Sentences are merged with too many commas. It's also confusing to string phrases along with commas, not indicating any order of importance:

> I couldn't sleep because it was too dark, and I was cold, plus my sister talked all night and she snored when she fell asleep, and the ground was hard.

Fixing Run-ons

Use the techniques below to turn run-ons into balanced, readable sentences.

Fix: Add a connecting word.
Run-on: We stayed up late we were watching the stars.
Fixed: We stayed up late **because** we were watching the stars.

Fix: Add punctuation.
Run-on: The veto is how the president the executive branch says no to a new law.
Fixed: The veto is how the president (the executive branch) says no to a new law.

Fix: Create two or more sentences.
Run-on: What I want is for us to help poor people I feel so sad when I see them on television.
Fixed: What I want is for us to help poor people. I feel so sad when I see them on television.

Sentence Fragments

A **fragment** is an incomplete sentence. It may start with a capital letter and have proper punctuation, but a fragment lacks a subject, a predicate, or both.

Fixing Fragments

Use these techniques to turn fragments into strong, complete sentences.

Fix: Add a noun or noun phrase.
Fragment: In Kentucky was born.
Fixed: Abraham Lincoln was born in Kentucky.

Fix: Add a verb or verb phrase.
Fragment: Later, Lincoln ending slavery.
Fixed: Later, Lincoln **debated** ending slavery.

Fix: Add a subject and a verb.
Fragment: Honest Abe, Father Abraham, and the Great Emancipator.
Fixed: People [subject] called [verb] him Honest Abe, Father Abraham, and the Great Emancipator.

Fix: Cut a connecting word.
Fragment: Because they thought he was a wise and capable leader.
Fixed: [Because] **T**hey thought he was a wise and capable leader.

FRAGMENTS BUILD MOOD!
Split-second scene described!

You should avoid sentence fragments in most writing situations, but sometimes fragments can help you express your ideas in unusual and interesting ways. In fiction and in sports reporting, for example, fragments can build moods or describe split-second action.

Mood: Drenching rain. Lightning. A falling tree. Crash! And then nothing more, until now, in this hospital bed.

Action: The quarterback pauses. Looking for an opening. Can't find it. Hunches down. Charges through. Flat on his back now, but over the goal line. And now a champion, at last.

Parallel Structure

In grammar, **parallel structures** have the same or similar construction. For example, the verbs *talked* and *ran* are parallel, because both verbs are in the past tense. The verbs *talked* and *are running* are not parallel, however, because they are in different tenses. Parallelism makes sentences more elegant and effective, as in the examples below.

Type of construction	Not parallel	Parallel
Multiple predicates	I **played** video games and **was watching** TV.	I **played** video games and **watched** TV.
Nouns in a series	Good sentences depend on **punctuation, word choice,** and **varying the structure.**	Good sentences depend on **punctuation**, **word choice**, and **variety of structure**.
One modifier referring to a series of nouns	For school I have **new** jeans, sweaters, and **bigger** shoes.	For school I have **new** jeans, sweaters, and shoes.
Phrases in a series	I sing **in** the shower, the breakfast table, and always **out of** tune.	I sing **in** the shower, **at** the breakfast table, and always **out of** tune.

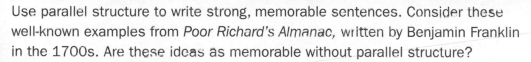

TIME Editors' Tip

Use parallel structure to write strong, memorable sentences. Consider these well-known examples from *Poor Richard's Almanac,* written by Benjamin Franklin in the 1700s. Are these ideas as memorable without parallel structure?

Not parallel	Parallel
When you **save** a **penny**, it is like you **earned** that **money.**	**A penny saved** is **a penny earned**.
Going to bed early and then **getting an early start** to the day will make you **feel better in many ways.**	**Early to bed** and **early to rise** makes a man **healthy**, **wealthy**, and **wise**.

Vary Your Sentences

Vary your sentences to give words more impact and keep the reader's interest. In the examples below, notice how changes to a sentence's length and structure cause other changes in emphasis, style, and tone.

Change the Length

Use sentences of different lengths to change your audience's reading pace and to vary the rhythm of your text. Short sentences move faster and can help you build suspense or make strong points. Long sentences give you room to add interesting details. They are also useful for creating moods, describing settings, and making lists.

Shorten sentences	Long	Shorter
Remove unnecessary adjectives and adverbs.	I'm usually sound asleep when the first light of dawn breaks.	I'm usually asleep when dawn breaks.
Remove unnecessary phrases and clauses.	As I often say, I really like pizza.	I really like pizza.
Restate phrases and clauses as single words.	My dad and mom met when they were in the same science class in college.	My parents met in a college science class.

Lengthen sentences	Short	Longer
Break a process into steps.	She made a peanut butter sandwich.	She cut a slice of bread, opened a jar of peanut butter, and made a sandwich.
Add descriptive details.	The trees change color in autumn.	In autumn, deciduous trees change from green to red and gold.
Add phrases and clauses.	Our team won the game.	The Fighting Tigers trailed in the first half but clawed their way to victory in the last quarter.

Change the Structure

Readers quickly lose interest in texts with boring, repetitive sentence structures. Changing the structure can shift emphasis to different words or alter the tone of the sentence. Use the strategies below to liven up your sentence structures and add interest to your writing.

Strategy: Rewrite sentences in different forms.
Original statement: We can pretend how it feels to fly.
Command: Imagine how it feels to fly.
Exclamation: Suddenly, you're flying!
Question: How would it feel to fly?

Strategy: Combine short sentences.
Original: Columbus went to sea as a young man. He sailed to many ports around the Mediterranean.
New: Columbus went to sea as a young man and sailed to many ports around the Mediterranean.

Strategy: Change the placement of clauses.
Original: Students listen to the principal when he speaks.
New: When the principal speaks, students listen.

TIME Editors' Tip

In all sentences, the subject noun and predicate verb must match, or agree: a singular subject takes the singular form of the verb, and a plural subject uses a plural verb form. Subject-verb disagreement often occurs in sentences that contain phrases or clauses. Here is a trick to help you discover whether your subjects and predicates agree. First, identify the potentially misleading phrase. Then, pretend it's not there. When this phrase disappears, you can more easily identify the sentence's actual subject and predicate and determine whether or not they agree.

The **number** [of portable stereo options] ~~increase~~ **increases** every year.

[Somewhere in this book] ~~are~~ **is** the **answers** to tomorrow's quiz.

Punctuation

When you speak, you pause frequently to take a breath or allow the listener to respond. Similarly, when you write you use punctuation marks to help the audience pace their reading and process meaning. **Punctuation marks** are symbols that show relationships among sentences, different parts of a sentence, or even individual words and parts of words in a sentence. When you use punctuation correctly, you will create a clear, coherent text for your readers.

The Purposes of Punctuation

Punctuation marks perform several different duties in a sentence.

- **End sentences.** Periods, question marks, and exclamation points show where a sentence ends. These punctuation marks also indicate whether a sentence is a statement, command, exclamation, or question.

- **Create pauses.** Other punctuation marks indicate pauses in the text. Commas are the most common of these marks, which also include colons, semicolons, parentheses, and dashes. Usually pauses separate sentence parts that may be confusing if read together. Pauses also help readers discern the most important and least important information in the sentence.

TIME Editors' Tip

When used wisely, punctuation marks help writers change their audience's experience of the text. Note the difference in the rhythm and intensity of the sentences below.

Without punctuation
When I arrived home at last I found a visitor relaxing on my couch even though I had neither invited him nor even let him know where I lived.

With punctuation
When I arrived home (at last!) I found a "visitor" relaxing on my couch—even though I had neither invited him nor even let him know where I lived.

- **Show quoted material.** Quotation marks indicate the exact words of a different writer or speaker. Quotations marks can also be used to show that a word or phrase is used ironically or humorously.

- **Show deleted material.** Finally, apostrophes and ellipses indicate where letters or words have been removed from a word or sentence. These marks help shorten a text or make its style less formal.

Periods

Use periods at the end of statements and commands.

Statement	I heard that this movie is excellent**.**
Command	Buy me some popcorn**.**

Periods may also occur in abbreviations and acronyms (an abbreviation made from the first letter of each word). In an abbreviation, the period usually occurs after the final letter. In an acronym the period is usually placed after the first letter of each shortened word.

Abbreviation	After living overseas, **Dr.** Potts is glad to be back in California.
Acronym	Luis has lived in the **U.S.A.** since he was born.

Not all abbreviations and acronyms take periods. For example, many company names, such as AT&T (American Telegraph and Telephone) and IBM (International Business Machines), do not use periods. Likewise, state postal abbreviations, such as AL (Alabama) and WV (West Virginia), do not take periods.

Exclamation Points

Use an exclamation point to signal a loud or emotional sentence or word.

Oh, this movie is horrible**!**
Wait**!** You forgot your homework**!**

Question Marks

Use a question mark to signal a question. In most questions the verb occurs before the subject. However, regular subject-verb statements and single words can become questions, too, when a question mark is placed at the end.

Do you want to leave**?**
What**?** My mom is here**?** Now**?**

Sometimes, question marks are used after parallel phrases to indicate a series of related questions.

Did you remember your book bag**?** Your lunch**?** Your math homework**?**

Commas

Commas are the most common punctuation marks in sentences. A comma always indicates a pause, but these pauses serve many different functions. In some cases, commas are needed to make a sentence's meaning clear. In others, commas change a sentence's tone or style.

Items in a Series: Use commas to separate a series of words or phrases that express a similar idea. Place a comma after each item in the series except the last one.

Beautiful beaches, warm weather, and lush plant life make Florida a fun vacation spot.
Its friendly people ask **who you are, where you are from,** and **what you like to do**.
Visit Florida's beaches to **swim in the surf, play in the sand, or lie in the sun**.

Place commas between a series of adjectives or adverbs when the meaning of the sentence does not change if the words are separated by *and*.

Florida's amusement parks offer **many [and] unique [and] exciting** activities.
Florida's amusement parks offer **many unique, exciting** activities.

Compound Sentences: A compound sentence contains two or more sentences connected by a conjunction, such as *and, but,* and *or*. Place a comma before the conjunction.

We moved to San Diego four years ago. I still miss my friends in Boston.
We moved to San Diego four years ago, **but** I still miss my friends in Boston.

However, do not use commas when the joined sentences are very short.

I ran. Will walked.
I ran and Will walked.

Think Again

One reason why writers have such difficulty with commas is that different texts use different rules for comma placement. This makes it difficult to learn exactly when a comma is necessary and when it is optional. For example, your Writer's Notebook says commas should occur after all but the last item in a series. However, to save space many newspapers and magazines do not use a comma between the last two items. The final choice is up to you, but whatever you choose to do, do it consistently or you may confuse your readers.

The final choice is yours.

Quotations: In a quotation, commas and quotation marks set off spoken or quoted words from the rest of the sentence. Where the comma is placed depends on where in the sentence the speaker is named.

Before	Molly suddenly burst out, "I have to get out of here!"
After	"There's no reason to yell," Sam calmly explained.
Both	"When we leave," she whispered, "let's go out the back door."

Beginning Phrases: Place a comma after a long or complicated phrase at the beginning of a sentence. A prepositional phrase consists of a preposition, such as *in* or *under*, plus its object. An adverbial phrase is a phrase that acts as an adverb in a sentence. A participial phrase contains the participial form of a verb.

Prepositional phrase	**With friends like you,** who needs enemies?
Adverbial phrase	**In your own words,** tell your story.
Participial phrase	**Thinking quickly,** I grabbed the envelope from his hands.

Unneeded Clauses: Some clauses can be cut from a sentence without changing the meaning. Others must remain for the sentence to make sense. Use commas to set off unnecessary clauses.

Commas needed	Henry Aaron, **who hit 755 home runs,** is a baseball legend.
No commas	He **who runs most swiftly** wins the race.
Commas needed	Our school, **which was built just last year,** has a leaking roof.
No commas	Knowing **which way is north** is an important hiking skill.

Directed Speech: Use commas to set off the name of someone who is directly spoken to.

Michael, will you grab that folder for me?
Which one, **Mr. Douglass**?
Give me the green one, **Michael,** next to your mouse pad.

Appositives: An appositive is a noun or noun phrase that explains another noun. Appositives are usually placed right after the nouns they explain. Use commas to set off an appositive.

The pope, **the head of the Roman Catholic Church,** lives in the Vatican.
Mr. Jones, **our biology teacher,** grades our homework fairly.

Interjections and Exclamations: An interjection is a word that expresses an emotion or sensation, such as *well* and *ouch*. An exclamation is a strongly emotional word or phrase, such as *hey* and *hurrah*. Use commas to set off these words whenever they occur.

Hey, be sure to send that e-mail before you leave!
Well, you should have told me earlier.
I did tell you about, **oh,** four hours ago.

Answers with Yes, No, or Maybe: Place commas after the words *yes*, *no*, and *maybe* when they begin sentences and answer direct or implied questions.

No, I didn't hear about the math test tomorrow. Will it be difficult?
Maybe, so we should meet after school to study.

Greetings: Place a comma between a word or phrase of greeting, such as *hello* or *what's up*, and the person being greeted. Also, place a comma after the greeting in a personal letter.

Greetings, earthlings.
What's up, Buttercup?
Dear Aunt Gloria and Uncle Steve, Thank you so much for your kind birthday present!

Abbreviations After Names: Place commas around abbreviations that follow a proper name, such as academic degrees, professional organizations, and *Jr.* and *Sr.*

Drew Pinsky, **M.D.,** will speak to our health class next week.
Cecile wrote her essay about Martin Luther King, **Jr.**

Locations and Addresses: Place commas after the name of a city and a state. Also, use commas to separate the street address, city, and state and zip code.

I lived in **Madison, Wisconsin,** for many years.
The Empire State Building is located at **350 Fifth Avenue, New York, NY 10118**.

Dates and Numbers: In dates, place a comma after the day of the month and the year. Always place a comma between two numbers that may otherwise be confused.

Juneteenth is a holiday that celebrates **June 19, 1865,** when enslaved Texans learned they were free.
Between 2000 and **2005, 357** of our former students graduated from college.

Semicolons

A semicolon works with commas to group long lists into shorter units.

> He runs, swims, or works out five hours a day; eats nothing but organically grown fruits, vegetables, and grains; and takes all kinds of vitamins.

You can also use a semicolon to separate a statement and a conclusion that can be drawn from it.

> Semicolons flourished when long sentences were in style; they became more rare when sentences grew shorter.

Colons

Use a colon before a list of items or actions.

> We've run out of these supplies: paper plates, paper cups, snacks, and soft drinks.

> Please do the following: go to the library, take out a cookbook, and bring it to me.

Colons are often used in two-part titles as well.

> *World Religions*: *An Introduction*

> "Faded Glory: Denim in America"

Think Again

Rules of punctuation are not set in stone; they change over time, just as speech does. Today, much of the information we read comes in bulleted lists. A **bullet** is a small dot or other symbol that calls attention to each item in a list. A colon often introduces the list. The bulleted items may form a complete sentence, or they may be individual phrases.

To play this game:
• insert the disk,
• select the play mode, and
• enter your initials.

Our school has many advantages:
• Small class sizes
• Sports teams
• College prep courses

Rules of punctuation are not set in stone.

Quotation Marks

Like commas, quotation marks set apart words within a sentence. Quotation marks always appear in pairs before and after a word, phrase, sentence, or group of sentences. Use quotation marks in the following situations:

A **direct quote** contains the exact words someone spoke or wrote. Direct quotes can record conversations or add an outside voice to a sentence.

"I think you and I are perfect together," he said.
As Shakespeare remarked, "All the world's a stage."

However, an indirect quote is one that is reworded by the writer. Indirect quotes *do not* take quotation marks.

Direct quote	"I will not raise taxes, no matter what happens," promised the president.
Indirect quote	The president promised he would not raise taxes under any circumstances.

Quotation marks are also used to **change the tone of a word or phrase.** The quotes signal to the reader that the writer is commenting on those words. Usually the writer's comment consists of sarcasm or irony.

The city's "improvements" included more parking lots, but no parks.

Finally, quotation marks indicate the **titles** of short works. These short works usually are part of a larger work or a collection of works, such as a book, album, television series, or magazine. (See page 23 for rules about italicizing the titles of longer works.)

Short story	"The Gift of the Magi"
Poem	"Dream Deferred"
Chapter	"The March to Yorktown"
Essay	"Bookshop Memories"
Newspaper or magazine article	"America's Best Public High Schools"
Song	"Purple Haze"
TV episode	"To Serve Man"

Quotation marks always appear in pairs, before and after words or phrases.

Apostrophes

An **apostrophe** replaces missing letters in a word. Contractions always contain an apostrophe.

> I **can't** make you do anything **you're** unwilling to do.

Apostrophes are also used to show possession or purpose. This table shows how apostrophes are used to create different kinds of possessives:

Singular noun	I like going to my **grandmother's house**.
Plural noun	The **cars' engines** started at once.
Collective noun	The book was a **children's story**.
Name that ends in *s*	Mrs. **Jones's dog** is smaller than the **Stevens's cat**.

Ellipses

An **ellipsis** is a series of three periods that take the place of words that have been cut from a sentence. Use an ellipsis to shorten a quote or to show interrupted speech. You can also use an ellipsis at the end of a sentence to create suspense.

Shorten a quote	We the people of the United States...do ordain and establish this Constitution for the United States of America.
Show interrupted speech	"It's just that I..." he muttered before falling silent.
Create suspense	I finally knew what had happened that night. At least, I thought I knew...

TIME Editors' Tip

Ellipses are a handy way to cut lenghty quotes down to size. However, be careful when you use ellipses that you do not change the meaning of the original quote. How do the ellipses change the meaning of the passage below? Is this a responsible use of ellipses?

Original

"Congress shall make no law respecting an establishment of religion, or prohibiting the free exercise thereof; or abridging the freedom of speech, or of the press; or the right of the people peaceably to assemble, and to petition the Government for a redress of grievances."

Misquote

"Congress shall make... law...abridging...the right of the people peaceably to assemble."

Parentheses

Parentheses surround information that, when removed, will still leave a complete sentence. Parentheses always come in pairs. Some parentheses occur within a sentence, while others occur between sentences. The text in the parentheses may be a phrase, a clause, or a complete sentence.

Like commas, parentheses may surround an appositive.

> I found my old teddy bear (the one I played with as a kid) up in the attic.

Parentheses may also contain the writer's or speaker's comments.

> Roger claims (you're not going to believe this) that he never went near the house.

One of the most important uses of parentheses is to cite sources of information.

> This idea was first developed by Albert Einstein in 1905 (Einstein 23).

You can also use parentheses to direct readers to other parts of a text.

> Some writers prefer to draft their work by hand rather than on a computer. (See Chapter 5 for more information.)

Dashes

A dash is a long horizontal mark that sets apart a group of words within a sentence. Dashes can take the place of commas, colons, or parentheses. Like exclamation points, they serve to emphasize ideas; therefore, they should not be overused. However, dashes are very useful for indicating sudden breaks in thought, creating suspense, or adding the punch line to a joke.

Break in thought	He promised me—not that you can believe a word he says—that I wouldn't have to go first.
Suspense	He crept up the stairs—slowly, silently, and with great fear—to investigate the strange noise.
Punch line	He's tough on the outside, soft on the inside, and often slightly cracked—in other words, he's a nut.

Parentheses and dashes set apart information in a sentence.

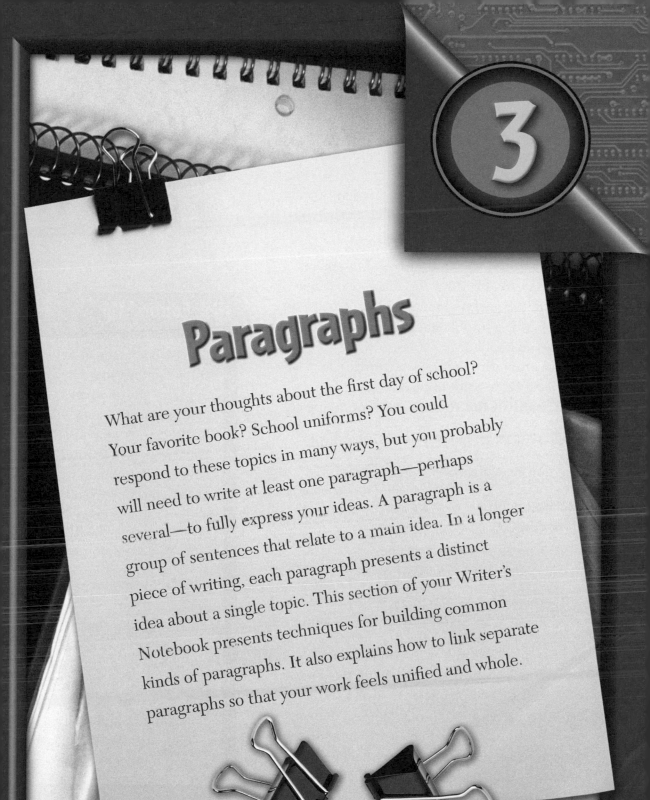

Paragraphs

What are your thoughts about the first day of school? Your favorite book? School uniforms? You could respond to these topics in many ways, but you probably will need to write at least one paragraph—perhaps several—to fully express your ideas. A paragraph is a group of sentences that relate to a main idea. In a longer piece of writing, each paragraph presents a distinct idea about a single topic. This section of your Writer's Notebook presents techniques for building common kinds of paragraphs. It also explains how to link separate paragraphs so that your work feels unified and whole.

Lead Paragraphs

Readers often decide if they will continue reading a work after only a few sentences, so first impressions are important. Good writers use compelling leads to draw readers into the text. A **lead** is the first paragraph in a longer work. Leads come in many forms, but a strong lead should do the following things:

- **Introduce the main idea** of the piece. In informal writing, the main idea can be implied, or stated indirectly. A formal lead contains a thesis sentence that clearly states the main point.
- **Capture the readers' attention** and make them want to read more.
- **Establish the tone** or "feel" of the piece.

Which paragraph below is the stronger lead?

> The first day of school is usually easy. Most years I just show up and get my books. Sometimes that's a lot harder than you think, though.

> I don't know why I was nervous, but I was. It certainly wasn't my first time walking into a new classroom. So why was the first day of ninth grade so much more difficult than all the first days before it?

The first lead introduces the topic, but readers are unlikely to continue reading a work that begins by expressing complaints or excuses. The second lead not only sets up the main idea, it does so in a way others can relate to—who hasn't been nervous when faced with a new challenge? Also, the honest tone makes readers believe that the author's ideas will be worth reading.

Use a Compelling lead!

TIME Editors' Tip

Like strong leads, good titles capture your readers' attention and give them a sense of what is to come. Make sure your titles give readers accurate information about your topic and inspire them to read on. Which titles below would you rather read?

"My Summer Vacation"
or
"Diving with the Dolphins at Waikiki"

"Learning to Drive"
or
"Whiplash and White Knuckles: My First Day at the Wheel"

Creating a Great Lead

A great lead grabs your audience's attention and draws them into your piece. Use the techniques below to launch your ideas into readers' lives.

A **compelling quote** tells readers that other persons of authority have ideas about your topic and that you recognize good writing when you see it.

> Aristotle once wrote, "It is the mark of an educated mind to be able to entertain a thought without accepting it." This mark is missing, however, in the rush to cut funding for after-school activities.

An **attention-getting statistic** shows the audience that your topic is important and worth investigating further.

> According to the American Lung Association, each day nearly 6,000 children under the age of 18 will start smoking, and nearly 2,000 of them will go on to become regular smokers. New programs seek to reduce these numbers by giving kids fun alternatives to smoking.

An **interesting example or anecdote** (personal story) can draw readers in with a compelling story or description.

> It was the final shot of the game. The basketball spun around and around the edge of the hoop until it slowed, stopped circling, and dropped into the net. Cheers rang out across the gymnasium. After four disappointing seasons, our team was finally going to the state tournament.

A **question that relates to readers' lives** shows that you have considered how your topic connects to problems or concerns that we all share.

> Have you ever said "yes" when you know you should have said "no"? When tenth-grader Justin Martin skipped Spanish class last Friday, he came to know this feeling all too well.

Nice to meet you!

Think Again

Many writers prefer not to use the word *you* in their work. However, using *you* in informal pieces can make the audience feel as if they're being spoken to directly. The text becomes more personal and readers respond with greater interest.

Thesis Sentences

What's the big idea? That's the question answered by a thesis sentence. **A thesis sentence** states a formal essay's main idea or argument. A good thesis sentence should do the following things:

Provide a clear and direct statement of the main idea. In the unclear example below, the author's position on the issue appears weak and uncertain.

Unclear	If soft drink machines are banned from schools, maybe they can be replaced with juice dispensers.
Clear	Soft drink machines should be banned from schools.

Make its point fully but succinctly. Don't hide your main idea in a forest of words.

Wordy	Homework is necessary because all learning can't take place in the classroom, but an overload of homework can cause some students to become burned out.
Succinct	Homework supports classroom learning, but too much homework can lead to burnout.

Occur at the beginning of the lead paragraph or the end of ement at the

beginning of the paragraph emphasizes supporting arguments. Placement at the end of the paragraph emphasizes the main idea.

Placed at the beginning	**Parents should consult with teens when setting curfews.** Teens know their own schedules better than parents. By having some control over their schedules, teens will be more likely to adhere to a curfew.
Placed at the end	Teens know their own schedules better than parents. By having some control over their schedules, teens will be more likely to adhere to a curfew. **As a result, parents should consult with teens when setting curfews.**

Think Again

Usually, the lead paragraph contains an essay's thesis sentence. Sometimes, though, a writer withholds the clearest statement of the main idea until the end of an essay. The writer builds up evidence within the essay's body and then places the thesis sentence in the conclusion as a final "knockout punch."

Body Paragraphs

The body of your essay or letter is where you really get to show the audience what you know. **Body paragraphs** provide the details, examples, and illustrations that back up the promise of information you made in the lead paragraph. All body paragraphs should follow a logical order and relate to the topic indicated in your lead.

Thesis statement	Prom night can be a memorable but expensive affair.
Topic sentence 1	Special clothes must be bought or rented for the event.
Topic sentence 2	Dinner at a nice restaurant is usually part of the evening.
Topic sentence 3	Flowers are traditional and add to the cost of prom night.

Topic Sentences

Each body paragraph should contain a **topic sentence** that tells readers what the paragraph is about. Each topic sentence should do the following:

Clearly state a paragraph's main point. Topic sentences, like your thesis sentence, help guide your readers through the text. This path should be clear of obstacles, such as unnecessary words. Make sure that each topic sentence develops a different aspect of the thesis statement.

Occur at or near the beginning of the paragraph. Such placement will prevent misunderstandings about the point of a paragraph.

Special clothes must be bought or rented for the event. For example, many teen girls have to purchase their prom dresses and accessories. Teen boys, however, often choose to rent tuxedoes. Either way, the cost can be substantial.

TIME Editors' Tip

JUST SAY IT!

Some writers worry that if they clearly state each topic sentence, their essays will become boring. Therefore, they prefer to imply or hint at their main points. Too often, though, this technique only hides the main idea from the audience. When it comes to topic sentences, just say it!

Transitions

Audiences enjoy reading texts that move easily from one idea to the next. **Transitions** are words and phrases that link separate paragraphs. The following techniques will move readers smoothly through your text and make them feel that your work is unified and whole.

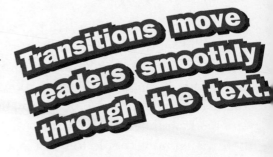

Repeat a key word or phrase. Echo what the audience has already read to move them smoothly on to new ideas.

Thesis sentence	Cats present a number of challenges to **pet owners**.
Paragraph 1	Among **pet owners**, cats have the reputation of being **finicky** eaters.
Paragraph 2	Cats are not only **finicky** about food, they can be very particular about their grooming as well.

Use a transitional word or phrase, such as *first, next, then, furthermore, finally, but, however, for example,* or *in addition to.* These devices help writers extend their discussion to new areas without jarring the reader.

Thesis sentence	Cats present a **number** of challenges to pet owners.
Paragraph 1	**First**, owners should be aware that cats are finicky eaters.
Paragraph 2	**Second**, grooming is an important part of a cat's life and a frequent chore for its owner as well.

TIME Editors' Tip

Transitions also help readers move smoothly between sentences. Note how transitional phrases and repeated words increase the readability of the sentences below.

Original
Owning pets can be a rewarding experience. They can provide companionship in a lonely home.

With transitions
Owning **pets** can be a **rewarding** experience. These **rewards** take several forms. **For example, pets** provide companionship in a lonely home.

Body Builders

Use the following techniques to build a variety of strong body paragraphs.

Add details. Details take your reader further into the paragraph's main idea.

Topic sentence	There are many opportunities to exercise and have fun during winter months.
Details	Depending on where you live, the winter sporting period may begin as early as October or as late as January. Many weather services provide special forecasts for outdoor athletes during these months. Consult these forecasts to find out more about how conditions can affect your safety and performance during winter activities.

Add examples. Examples help establish your authority on a topic. Readers who already know something about your topic want to see that you have sufficient knowledge to speak to them. Less-informed readers will understand your ideas better if you provide concrete examples.

Topic sentence	There are many opportunities to exercise and have fun during winter months.
Examples	Winter sports, like skiing and snowboarding, provide fun ways to exercise outdoors. But if you prefer to stay inside, basketball is a good indoor sport. If you play basketball at a gym or fitness center, you can also take classes or work out on the weightlifting and exercise equipment.

TIME Editors' Tip

In sports and in writing, sometimes it is necessary to make direct contact. When adding details or using examples to build body paragraphs, be sure these ideas relate to the paragraph's topic sentence and to the essay as a whole. **Digressions** are ideas that lead away from the main idea of an essay or paragraph, and they should be avoided. If the idea is truly important, put it in its own paragraph!

Compare and contrast. You can present a balanced view of your topic by showing how ideas are alike or different. Always remember to compare and contrast things that relate to each other by kind (what they are) or degree (how much or how little).

Topic sentence	There are many opportunities to exercise and have fun during winter months.
Compare by kind	Downhill sports such as skiing and snowboarding require special—and often expensive—equipment. Boots, poles, skis, and snowboards must all be chosen according to your body type or snow conditions. Rentals are available on some items, but such equipment may affect your safety and performance.
Compare and contrast by degree	Favorites such as skiing and snowboarding provide a thrilling experience and stunning winter scenery. However, some people prefer less dangerous outdoor activities. Cross-country skiing is a strenuous but safe way to see snow-clad peaks and valleys. Hiking can take outdoor enthusiasts through similar areas, but at a more leisurely pace.

Show cause and effect. Identify causes and their effects to help readers analyze processes and decisions related to your topic.

Topic sentence	There are many opportunities to exercise and have fun during winter months.
Causes and effects	If you choose skiing as a winter sport, you will need extra money to pay for special clothing and equipment. For downhill skiing, you will also have the extra expense of lift tickets. Hiking is an inexpensive outdoor activity that will allow you to have extra money to save or spend on something else that you enjoy. You also will reduce the chances of injury associated with downhill skiing.

Essays, Letters, and Résumés

You can't get away from it—writing is a part of your life. You write essays in school; letters and e-mails to friends, family, and businesses; and résumés for a job interview. To perform these tasks successfully, you must understand what readers expect from you in each situation. This section of your Writer's Notebook explains common forms of student writing. It also includes tips for getting started and a complete example of each form. Remember, good writing knows no bounds. The skills you need to write successfully in one situation will help you succeed in other writing situations, too.

Common Forms of Student Writing

Students use a wide variety of writing forms, from informal texts such as class notes and text messages, to formal texts such as essay exams and research reports. Most of your formal writing tasks, however, take one of three forms: an essay, a letter, or a résumé.

Essays

Most of your writing assignments in school are essays. An **essay** is a short composition that is used to inform, explain, or persuade. Essays are useful in communicating opinions, discovering facts through research, and showing different views on a subject. You will mainly write five kinds of essays:

- A **narrative essay** relates a real-life story, often a personal experience.

- A **literature response essay** explains your reaction to a text.

- An **expository essay** presents information about a topic and often requires research.

- A **persuasive essay** convinces others to agree with your position on an issue.

- A **college entry essay** introduces you to the admissions board of a college or university and explains why you should be accepted to study at their school.

Every writing assignment takes into account three things: the subject (what is written about), the audience (to whom the work is written), and the author himself or herself (who is writing and what is their personal style). This is called the **writing triangle**. In successful writing assignments, all three points of the triangle work together. For example, if you write about a topic that excites you, the topic will be enthusiastically described and your audience will read the work with interest. However, a topic that bores you is unlikely to receive your best writing and so your readers may be bored, too. (For more about the writing triangle, see page 98 of your Writer's Notebook.)

Résumés

A **résumé** is a document that highlights your experience to a potential employer. It includes your work history, education, and volunteer work. Unlike essays and letters, résumés often consist of lists rather than complete paragraphs. There are two common kinds of résumés:

- A **chronological résumé** presents your employment history in order of occurrence.

- A **functional résumé** presents your experience as a set of specific skills.

A résumé is usually sent with another document called a **cover letter.** This is a formal letter that introduces you to the employer and states the reasons for your interest in his or her business.

Successful letters use the same set of writing skills, regardless of how they are sent.

Letters

A **letter** is a document written and sent to a specific person or group. Students usually write two kinds of letters:

- A **personal letter** is an informal document written to family or friends.

- A **business letter** is a formal document written to a person or persons in a company, government, or other organization.

E-mail has replaced the postal service as the preferred way for sending many kinds of letters. However, successful letters use the same set of writing skills and formatting strategies, regardless of how they are sent.

Get Started

The first step in any writing assignment is to figure out what is to be written and how. Read or listen carefully to all instructions. Don't be afraid to ask questions the moment you don't understand any part of an assignment. The answers to these questions will keep you on the right track and save you from having to rework your writing unnecessarily.

Narrative Essay

A **narrative essay** tells a story about an event or situation. It is often written in the first person (using *I* and *me*), with the author reflecting on what happened and what he or she has learned as a result. The best narrative essays *show* the event or incident as it happened in vivid details, rather than just *tell* the audience about it. The techniques described here will help you bring your personal experiences to life for your readers.

Use Fiction Techniques

Narrative essays are nonfiction works, but you can use the elements of fiction to tell your true-life tales.

Characters are the people in a fictional story or narrative essay. Strong, realistic characters draw readers in and move the story forward. Remember, descriptions of characters are important, but **dialogue** allows readers to learn about your characters from their own words.

Okay	Ricardo was a shy, new kid in class. He had just moved here from Mexico.
Better	"*Hola*, I am Ricardo," said a soft voice. "Do you mind if I sit here?"

Setting is the place and time of your narrative. A setting doesn't have to be striking or strange to attract readers. Instead, try describing familiar settings in new ways.

Okay	The small stone and wood church was built in 1910.
Better	I entered the tiny, crumbling church and was met by the smell of wood polish and wet stone.

Plot is the organization of a narrative into a beginning, middle, and end. Each part of the plot plays a different role in the story. Use the plot structure below to present readers with a complete and satisfying essay about your experiences.

Beginning	Draws readers in; introduces characters, setting, and problem
Middle	Develops characters, setting, and problem
End	Resolves problem; shows how characters and setting have changed

The "Sense" of a Story

A narrative essay should include many sensory descriptions. These details make readers feel as if they are part of the narrative. Be sure to use all five senses, as in the example below.

Smell	The wind blew across my face and brought with it the fragrance of saltwater and fish, not everyone's kind of perfume.
Sound	Seagulls screeched overhead.
Sight	Boats with rainbow-colored sails danced across water so blue that I couldn't tell where sky and water met.
Taste	I bit into the peanut butter and jelly sandwich, the sweetness marred by the gritty taste of sand.
Touch	Sharp stones poked my feet as I stumbled into the warm water.

Notice how concrete nouns and vivid, precise verbs help readers share in the author's experience at the beach. They also tell readers that the author is a skilled observer. Whatever happens next in the narrative, readers will have a strong understanding of where and to whom it happened because of these keenly observed and well-written details.

Get Started

To begin writing a narrative essay, pick several events from your journal or your memory. These don't have to be special occasions, such as birthdays or graduations. Everyday events, such as challenges to overcome or changes in your routine, can also affect you in important ways. Now ask these questions to discover which event you may want to share with others:

- **Do you have new insight or knowledge because of the event?**

- **Does the event have the elements of a strong narrative?**

- **Does the event provide enough material to write an essay of the proper length?**

If you answer yes to these questions, then the event could be a good subject for a narrative essay.

Narrative Essay Example

Strong title

At the Crossroads

The four-door Chevrolet was still new, but that "new car" smell had been replaced by the "new driver" odor of nervous sweat. I had excitedly signed up for driver's education with my best friend Marcie. Now, though, I doubted my judgment.

Plot beginning, with sense descriptions

George, the other person in our group, had just clipped a mailbox, scraping the passenger-side mirror. The suburban neighborhood had rural-type mailboxes by the curb, and each one tried to grab us as George steered past.

Identification and description of characters and setting

"It's better to scrape our mirror than a parked car." Coach Fisher's voice was calm. "Next time, George, just ease into the lane after you've passed a parked car."

When Coach Fisher wasn't teaching us how to avoid mailboxes, he coached our championship basketball team. His easygoing confidence helped both the team and his driving students handle stress. Still, my heart beat as fast as a hummingbird's wings.

Marcie traded places with George. My best friend stomped on the accelerator, slamming our bodies back in our seats, and the Chevy galloped down the street. At the corner, Marcie skidded to a stop, the brakes squealing in protest. Our bodies lurched forward.

Vivid verbs

"Take it easy, Marcie," Coach Fisher advised. "We're not in a race." By the end of her session, her lead foot had lightened up.

My turn arrived. Since my parents had worked with me before I signed up for this class, I had mastered the basics of street driving. So why could I taste my lunch all over again? I knew what was coming next.

Plot middle, with development of problem

1

We were at a four-way stop when Coach Fisher said the dreaded words. "Turn left and get on the freeway."

I could hear both George and Marcie sucking in their breath. Beads of sweat popped out on my forehead and I felt faint. This is where my parents had chickened out. They loved me, but not enough to get on the freeway with me in the driver's seat. And now George's run-in with the mailbox had spooked me, too.

Still stopped at the crossroads, I said, "I can't do it."

"Have you ever tried before?" Coach Fisher asked.   • **Dialogue**

"No."

"Then how do you know you can't do it?" he asked me patiently. "You've been doing new things since you took your first breath. This will be just one more."

"But what if I get into an accident?"

"What if you *don't*?" He smiled confidently at me. "Instead of imagining disaster, visualize driving successfully on the freeway. I think you're ready, but if you don't agree, then turn right."

If I turned right, I could continue driving down suburban streets with my learner's permit, but I would never get my license. I'd have to rely on my unreliable older sister to take me places. If I turned left, I • **Concrete nouns** would drive onto the scary freeway with its rushing traffic. I closed my eyes for a moment and saw myself driving without incident on that eight-lane monster.

The monster had to be conquered sooner or later. Taking a deep • **Plot end, with problem resolved** breath, I put on the turn signal, eased my foot off the brake, and turned left.

2

Literature Response Essay

Good writers read a lot, and they want to share ideas about what they have read with others. A **literature response essay** presents your reaction to something you have read. Literature in this case means any written work, whether it is a novel, a newspaper editorial, or a chapter from one of your textbooks.

Kinds of Responses

Think of a literature response essay as one half of an ongoing conversation between the author and you, a member of the author's audience. To hold up your end of the conversation, you can do the following things:

- **Study** the information in the reading. What new information does the author offer? Are the facts really true? Is the evidence convincing? Are the characters true to life?

- **Compare** the reading to other works. How is this reading like or unlike other readings? What is the cause of these differences?

- **Analyze** the author's choices. How does the author organize the work? What information is included, and why? What information is left out, and why?

- **Question** the author's purpose. What is significant about this reading? What purpose does it serve? What biases does the author have toward the topic?

- **React** emotionally to the reading. How does the reading make you feel? Which emotions is the author trying to activate in his or her audience?

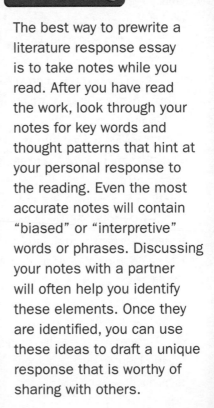

Get Started

The best way to prewrite a literature response essay is to take notes while you read. After you have read the work, look through your notes for key words and thought patterns that hint at your personal response to the reading. Even the most accurate notes will contain "biased" or "interpretive" words or phrases. Discussing your notes with a partner will often help you identify these elements. Once they are identified, you can use these ideas to draft a unique response that is worthy of sharing with others.

Elements of a Strong Response

To write a successful literature response essay, be sure to do the following things:

Identify the author and title of the work. The first time you identify the author, use his or her full name. After the first mention, use only the last name.

> In "The Homework Ate My Family" (*TIME Magazine*, January 25, 1999), Romesh Ratnesar discusses the stress that homework puts on students and their families.

Show understanding of the reading's main ideas by restating them in your own words.

> He believes that the time families spend on homework should be spent developing family relationships. In most families, both parents have jobs and would rather spend homework time playing with their kids.

Interpret the work's structure and style. These acts of interpretation truly show your unique response to a reading. Structural interpretation usually describes where information is given, and why. Stylistic interpretation usually describes how, or in what form, information is given, and why. In both cases, you should note the effect of these decisions on the reader.

> Ratnesar uses statistics and interviews with children and their parents to make his point that homework is taking up too much family time. The statistics are especially convincing. They prove that homework is at least partly to blame for the time crunch, along with longer working hours for parents and more time spent watching television.

Include evidence from the reading to support your interpretation. That way, readers will know that you are basing your interpretation on the work itself and not on your own biases.

> For example, Ratnesar notes that researchers at the University of Michigan have shown that the average amount of time spent weekly on homework has gone up from 2 hours 49 minutes to more than 3½ hours.

Read the essay below, then note a reader's response on the facing page.

Saving America's Soul Kitchen
by Wynton Marsalis

Now the levee breach has been fixed. The people have been evacuated. Army Corps of Engineers magicians will pump [New Orleans] dry, and the slow (but quicker than we think) job of rebuilding will begin.... Americans of all stripes will demonstrate saintly concern for one another. It's what we do in a crisis.

This tragedy, however, should make us take an account of ourselves.... Let us assess the size of this cataclysm in cultural terms, not in dollars and cents or politics. That's what the city of New Orleans can now teach the nation again.... I say teach us again, because New Orleans is a true American melting pot: the soul of America.... Whites, Creoles and Negroes were strained, steamed and stewed in a thick, sticky, below-sea-level bowl of musky gumbo. These people produced an original cuisine, an original architecture, vibrant communal ceremonies and an original art form: jazz....

The images of a ruined city make it clear that we need to rebuild New Orleans. The images of people stranded, in shock, indicate that we need to rebuild a community. The images of all sorts of Americans aiding these victims speak of the size of our hearts. But this time we need to look a little deeper. Let's use the resurrection of the city to reacquaint the country with the gift of New Orleans: a multicultural community invigorated by the arts.... Our democracy from its very beginnings has been challenged by the shackles of slavery.... Not fixing the city's levees before Katrina struck will now cost us untold billions. Not resolving the nation's issues of race and class has and will cost us so much more.

Wynton Marsalis, the jazz trumpeter ... was born and raised in New Orleans.

"Saving America's Soul Kitchen," by Wynton Marsalis (*TIME Magazine*, September 19, 2005, page 84).

The Message of New Orleans

In "Saving America's Soul Kitchen" (TIME magazine, September 19, 2005), Wynton Marsalis uses the city of New Orleans as a symbol of the way the United States should be, but isn't. Marsalis is a jazz musician who was born and raised in New Orleans, so he knows the city well and displays his knowledge in this essay. He has seen firsthand how people from many different backgrounds have worked together to create a city that many people claim as their favorite.

Identification of author and title

Marsalis describes New Orleans as a multicultural city that emphasizes originality in the arts, such as food, architecture, and music. He says that this originality comes from a unique "melting pot" in which different cultures were "strained, steamed, and stewed in a thick, sticky, below-sea-level bowl of musky gumbo." He concludes by saying that as we rebuild New Orleans after the disaster of Hurricane Katrina, we should also rebuild our attitudes toward each other. The problems of race and class won't be resolved until we do.

Sound understanding of main ideas

Use of evidence to support interpretation

By using New Orleans as a symbol of what America could someday be, Marsalis helps the reader understand his message without pointing fingers at specific persons or parties or races. It's not until the very end of his essay that Marsalis brings up racism and how it has hurt our nation for hundreds of years, and how America still hasn't resolved all the problems racism has produced. He makes a good point in a way that causes the reader to agree and want to help fix the problem.

Analysis of style (symbolism)

Analysis of structure (organization)

Expository Essay

In an **expository essay,** the writer explains a topic, defines a term, or gives up-to-date information. These essays are often called research reports, because the writer usually searches out information about his or her topic in a library, on the Internet, or from other resources. The information on the following pages will help you research, organize, and document a variety of expository essays.

Kinds of Expository Essays

Each expository essay below presents your audience with a specific kind of information and organization:

- A **historical essay** is about a person or event from the past. These essays are usually organized by the order of events. However, be careful not to turn the essay into a boring list of dates. A successful historical essay is like a good story that shows readers what it was like to know a person or witness an event from long ago.

- A **current events essay** is about an issue, person, or event that is now in the news. You do not present your personal opinion about the topic. Instead you explain why people think the issue is important and describe their different points of view. Sometimes a current events essay is organized chronologically. Other times, you will organize these essays around people who are for and against an issue, or around the benefits (pros) and risks (cons) of a proposed action.

- A **process essay** describes how to do something. For example, scientists often write process essays to describe how they performed an experiment. Process essays also can be used for everyday purposes, such as giving friends directions to your house. Use the steps it takes to complete the process to organize this kind of essay.

- A **definition essay** gives the reader information about the unique features of a topic. For example, an essay about African elephants tells readers what makes these animals different from other animals. Organize a definition essay around important features of your topic. For an essay about African elephants, these main ideas may include physical characteristics such as body parts and size, and behaviors such as habitat and diet.

Explain a topic, define a term, or give up-to-date information!

Elements of Exposition

Most expository essays have a set format and use a formal tone. Use the elements below to guide your work:

- Think of the **lead paragraph** in an expository essay as a compass that shows the reader the way to go. Begin your lead with an eye-catching statistic, quote, or example. Then write a clear, direct thesis statement that says what the essay will be about. This thesis statement will help keep you and your audience from wandering away from the essay's focus.

- The **body paragraphs** present the main points and evidence that support the thesis statement. Each paragraph contains one main point with supporting evidence. In a longer essay, body paragraphs may be grouped under **subheadings** that help readers keep track of where they are in the text.

- The **conclusion** ties together the essay's main ideas and re-emphasizes the importance of the topic to the audience.

- **Documentation** occurs throughout an expository essay and takes two forms. A **citation** is a note in the text that identifies your source for a quote, statistic, or unique idea. The **Works Cited page** occurs at the end of your essay and lists complete publication information for each of your sources. (See pages 68–71 for more information about when and how to cite your sources.)

Get Started

To choose an appropriate topic for your expository essay, first identify a general area of interest, such as skateboarding. Then ask yourself, "What do I already know about this topic?" List the information you know, such as the difference between shortboards and longboards. Then ask, "What do I *want* to know?" Perhaps you are curious about how different kinds of skateboards came about. Who invented them? When? Why? As you research your topic, ask yourself "What have I learned?" Then answer this question to create a first draft of your expository essay.

Finding Information

For most expository essays, the writer will perform **research** to find sources of information. Depending on your topic, this research may take you to a library, a media center, or even someone's living room. Use a variety of sources from those listed below to find accurate, balanced information about your topic:

- **Books** usually provide the most in-depth information about your topic, so you should begin looking for appropriate titles early in your research. Depending on your topic, these books may include fiction works, such as novels and short story collections, or nonfiction works, such as biographies, histories, and collections of articles. Reference books, such as general and special-interest encyclopedias, are a good first stop for any researcher.

- **Periodicals** are works that come out in issues, such as newspapers and magazines. Because periodicals are published more frequently than books, they often contain the most up-to-date information about a topic.

- **Audio-visual media**—such as movies, television programs, and music albums—can be sources of information, too. Even if your topic does not directly relate to these media, they are great places to find compelling quotes and interesting examples to use in your essay's lead.

- **The Internet** is now the world's largest research tool. Most companies, organizations, schools, and governments have Web sites, many of which contain large amounts of information. Periodicals and books are also increasingly available online. Keep in mind, however, that people can post information on the Internet regardless of whether or not they are experts in the field. Always make sure that a qualified person or group has posted the information. Web addresses ending in .gov or .edu are usually among the most reliable Internet resources.

- **Interviews** are a great way to get firsthand information about your topic. Don't be shy! Many people enjoy talking about their work or their role in an important event.

Get Started

Librarians are perhaps the most valuable research tools of all! They are experts in finding information and are very helpful in directing you to a wide range of source materials, some of which you may not have realized were available.

Taking Notes

Note-taking is an important research skill. Without good notes, the information you've gathered can be quickly lost in a pile of books, photocopies, and printouts. Use the techniques below to keep your information organized and at hand:

- **Use note cards** to record information from and about your sources. This is an old-fashioned technique that still works. Note cards are portable, so you can take them to libraries and other places where information is stored. Also, you can use the note cards to help organize your essay by shuffling and sorting the cards into the order their information will appear in your draft.

- **Note *all* important source information.** You will need this information for your citations and Works Cited page. (See pages 69–71 for the information you should record for each kind of source.) Also, assign each source a number; after you have recorded complete information on the first card for a source, you can simply write the source number at the top of each additional card.

- **Note the source's location in the library.** This information is your roadmap back to a source, in case you need to revisit it later.

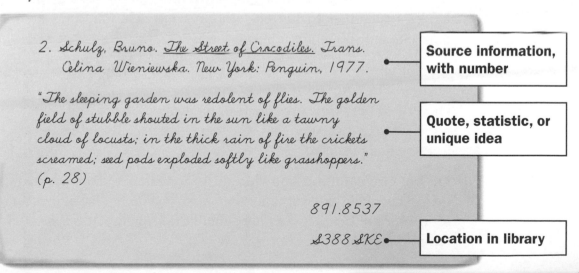

2. Schulz, Bruno. *The Street of Crocodiles.* Trans. Celina Wieniewska. New York: Penguin, 1977.

Source information, with number

"The sleeping garden was redolent of flies. The golden field of stubble shouted in the sun like a tawny cloud of locusts; in the thick rain of fire the crickets screamed; seed pods exploded softly like grasshoppers." (p. 28)

Quote, statistic, or unique idea

891.8537
S388 SKE

Location in library

Documentation Guide

Documentation, or giving credit to your sources, is an important part of an expository essay. Used properly, documentation helps readers trust your information. There are many ways to document your work, but the MLA (Modern Language Association) style outlined in your Writer's Notebook works well in most situations. The MLA style information on the following pages will help you document expository essays accurately and responsibly.

When to Cite

A **citation** is a note that lets readers know when evidence occurs in your essay and tells them from where it came. Use the guidelines below to help you decide when to include a citation in your essay:

- **Cite exact quotes or statistics.** The only exception to this rule is when the quote or statistic is already widely known. For example, you do not have to cite the fact that there are 50 states or that Dorothy in *The Wizard of Oz* said, "There's no place like home."

- **Cite a conclusion or unique idea.** Cite the source for any statement that could be debated, unless the statement is your own idea. For example, you do not have to cite the fact that gasoline is made from petroleum. But if an author states that the use of petroleum products is the biggest environmental problem in the United States, then that is the author's own conclusion, and you must cite it if you report it in your essay.

- **Do not cite facts that are widely known by people who write about your topic.** For example, most historians already know the order of the presidents of the United States. You would not need to cite a source that tells you George W. Bush was the forty-second president.

- **Do not cite common knowledge.** Your readers will already know many facts about the world. For example, you do not have to cite a source for the fact that the president of the United States is elected rather than appointed.

How to Cite

In MLA style, cite your source in parentheses at the end of a sentence.

When the author's name is in the text, cite the page number of the source where the quote or information is found.

> According to Thomas Hines, author of *I Want That!*, "Most people are learning to shop before they can read a word" **(5)**.

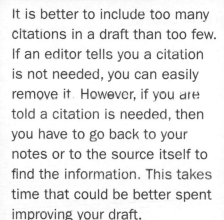

TIME Editors' Tip

It is better to include too many citations in a draft than too few. If an editor tells you a citation is not needed, you can easily remove it. However, if you are told a citation is needed, then you have to go back to your notes or to the source itself to find the information. This takes time that could be better spent improving your draft.

When the source's author is not named in the text, include his or her last name in the citation. If the work has no author, use the title. Shorten the title if it is more than a few words long.

> The United States has the largest economy in the world **(New York Times Almanac 515)**.

> In fact, "Never before have so many people been able to buy so many things" **(Hines 19)**.

Identify secondhand quotes by adding the phrase *qtd. in*.

> "Usually I buy something that I feel guilty about, just something that I've got three or four of at home," noted one woman in a study of shopping habits **(qtd. in Hines 109)**.

If you cite more than one work by the same author, include a shortened title in the citation. The book cited below is Thomas Hines's *The Rise and Fall of the American Teenager*.

> Young Americans also spend billions of dollars every year on clothing and entertainment **(Hines American Teenager 7)**.

How to Create a Works Cited Page

The **Works Cited page** of your expository essay lists all the sources you cited in your text. Use the rules and formatting information below to create this important page:

- **List the sources in alphabetical order** by author. If the author is unknown, then alphabetize the source by the first important word in the title. (Ignore *A, An,* or *The* at the beginning of the title.)

- **List every source you used in your essay.** If you cited a work in your text, it must appear as an entry on your Works Cited page.

- **Do not indent the first line of the entry.** If the entry extends past one line, then indent the following line or lines two or three spaces from the left margin.

Books and Parts of Books	
Basic Style	Last name, First name, Middle initial. *Title.* City: Publisher, Year.
One author	Palladino, Grace. *Teenagers: An American History.* New York: Basic, 1996.
Two authors	Kenny, Maureen E., and Laura A. Gallagher. *Teenagers and Community Service: A Guide to the Issues.* Westport, CT: Praeger, 2003.
Edited collection	Burns, Kate, ed. *The American Teenager.* San Diego: Greenhaven, 2003.
Part of an edited collection	Cooper, B. Lee, "Popular Music Reflects Teens' Attitudes About School." *The American Teenager.* Ed. Kate Burns. San Diego: Greenhaven, 2003. 194–202.
Translated book	Baudrillard, Jean. *America.* Trans. Chris Turner. New York: Verso, 1986.
No author	*Webster's Ninth New Collegiate Dictionary.* Springfield, MA: Merriam-Webster, 1984.

Periodical Articles	
Basic Style	Last name, First name, Middle initial. "Article Title." *Publication* Date: Pages.
Magazine article	Wallis, Claudia. "What Makes Teens Tick." *TIME Magazine* 10 May 2004: 56–65.
Newspaper article	Kampert, Patrick. "Frantic Lives Trigger Teen Depression." *Chicago Tribune* 25 Sept. 2005: 1Q.
Article from online database	Joyce, Colin. "Teens Today." *Society* 11 Nov. 2005: 12. LexisNexis Academic. 20 Dec. 2005. <http://www.lexisnexis.com/academic/>
Media and Other Sources	
Web site	"Best Books for Young Adults 2005." Young Adult Library Services Association. 17 Oct. 2005. <http://www.ala.org/ala/yalsa/yalsa.htm>
Television program	"Inside the Teenage Brain." *Frontline.* PBS. WTTW, Chicago. 31 Jan. 2001.
Music recording	Radiohead. "Creep." *Pablo Honey.* Capitol, 1993.
Film	*I Was a Teenage Werewolf.* Dir. Herman Cohen. American International, 1957.
Interview	Loesch, Rebecca. Personal interview. 8 May 2006.

TIME Editors' Tip

The MLA documentation information on these pages covers the most common sources used by student writers. However, if you need to cite a source that is not listed here, you can often find the proper style by searching the Internet. Many universities post online information about how to format sources in MLA style.

The Wright Stuff:
The Wright Brothers and the First Airplane

Strong title

It all started with a simple toy. In 1878, when Wilbur Wright was eleven years old and his brother Orville was seven, their father brought home a gift that would change their lives and that of the world. Bishop Milton Wright concealed a toy in his hands, then tossed it in the air. Years later, the brothers recalled that the toy "flew across the room till it struck the ceiling, where it fluttered awhile, and finally sank to the floor" (Wright "Aeroplane"). The boys were fascinated with this toy, playing with it until it broke, and then making their own versions. The Wright brothers' boyhood interest in flight would continue for years until, in 1903, they invented the world's first manned, motorized airplane.

Introduction contains interesting story

Quote and citation

Clear thesis sentence

Handy Boys

Subheadings show the organization of body paragraphs.

The Wright brothers were handy at building many different things. Orville built kites for neighborhood boys and later built a printing press. Wilbur built a paper-folding machine for his father's church newsletter. Later, they helped build a porch onto the family home and installed a fireplace in the parlor (Howard 10).

Orville left high school early, and together with his brother and a close friend started a print shop. They produced a neighborhood weekly newspaper, where they occasionally printed aeronautical news. From the printing business, the brothers turned to repairing bicycles. Later, the Wrights began building their own bicycles. They also built an engine to drive their workshop machinery (Freedman 13). All this building and inventing was preparing the brothers for their next step: flight!

Paragraphs are organized by order of events, because this is a history essay.

1

A Growing Interest

Over time, what had started as a curiosity became a passion for flying machines. The Wright brothers studied what others had done and noticed that most had not paid much attention to control of their gliders (Howard 12). In the bicycle shop, Orville and Wilbur built an unmanned, biplane glider with a five-foot wingspan to be flown like a kite. Theirs was the only bicycle shop where "wings [were] being built as well as wheels" (Gates 24).

After watching a flock of pigeons one day, the brothers realized the birds moved the tips of their wings to maintain balance (Howard 33). Playing with an inner tube box, Wilbur figured out how to make the wings of their biplane twist like a bird's wing. When they tested their biplane in 1900, it worked perfectly. They next wanted to test their ideas with a manned flight.

Because the bicycle business was financing their flight experiments, Oliver and Wilbur needed to keep the shop open. They could only test a manned flight between September and January, when the bicycle season slowed down. Their friend, Octave Chanute, suggested that they test their biplane in a sandy area for a softer landing. They chose Kitty Hawk, South Carolina, for its stretches of sandy beach.

First Attempts

Before making the trip to South Carolina in the fall of 1900, Wilbur wrote to his father, "It is my belief that flight is possible, and while I am taking up the investigation for pleasure rather than profit, I think there is a slight possibility of achieving fame and fortune from it" (qtd. in Freeman 32).

Clear topic sentence

Citations occur throughout the essay.

Subheadings occur at logical points in the story.

Proper citation for second-hand quote

2

Fame and fortune would have to wait a few years, however. The brothers' 17-foot biplane had no motor, and they planned to fly it like a kite, but with a man inside controlling it. They hauled the biplane down the beach to a group of dunes called Kill Devil Hills, and as Wilbur lay inside, the wind lifted the craft like a bird. Those first flights lasted a mere 20 seconds and only traveled about 300 feet, but it proved that the Wrights' basic design worked.

The next year, 1901, the brothers built a glider with a wingspan of 22 feet. The bigger glider, however, didn't respond as the smaller one had because of problems with the wings and the controls. After they returned home to Dayton, the brothers discovered a major error in their calculations. They corrected the error, built a wind tunnel to test a new model, and then built another glider.

The 1902 glider worked even better than expected! The glider spent most of the time at Kill Devil Hills in the air. There were still some problems, but most of the major difficulties had been solved. The next step was to build an airplane with a motor.

Success at Last

Back home in Dayton, the brothers began working on their first powered airplane. They developed a lightweight, 12-horsepower engine. They also used their bicycling knowledge to design a transmission system for twin propeller blades. For the launch, the Wrights designed a rail system so the plane could gain the momentum it needed to become airborne. All that was left to do was see if their motor-driven airplane would actually work.

Proper format for numbers in measurements

Compare-contrast paragraph

Transitions between body paragraphs

3

When the brothers arrived at Kill Devil Hills on Tuesday, December 15, 1903, they tossed a coin to see who would get the first ride. Wilbur won the toss, but his flight crashed after only 3½ seconds. Two days later, the plane was ready to go again, this time with Orville at the controls. "This flight lasted only 12 seconds," Orville said later, "but it was nevertheless the first in the history of the world" (Freedman 76). Each brother flew several more times, with Wilbur making the longest flight of 59 seconds over 852 feet. The Wright brothers had done it! After years of trying, they had designed and flown the world's first airplane.

A Future in the Air

It was 21 years after that historic first flight that Orville attended an air show at the Wilbur Wright Field near Dayton, Ohio, where many different planes lined the runway. "As I stand . . . where our earlier experiments were conducted and see how the principles of flight we used 21 years ago are still being used, I am extremely proud." (qtd. in "Dayton" 1). And he should have been proud. What had started as the curiosity of two boys became the success story of two dedicated people who began the era of human flight and changed our world forever.

Final quote and citation

Conclusion summarizes the essay.

4

Center Works Cited
at top of the page.

Works Cited

"At Dayton." *TIME* 13 Oct. 1924: 70.

Freedman, Russell. *The Wright Brothers: How They Invented the Airplane.* New York: Holiday House, 1991.

Gates, Bill. "The Wright Brothers." *TIME* 29 March 1999: 97.

Howard, Fred. *Wilbur and Orville: A Biography of the Wright Brothers.* New York: Alfred A. Knopf, 1987.

5

Use proper
MLA style for
each source.

Indent entries
after first line.

Alphabetize sources
by author and title.

The Wright Brothers Memorial atop Kill Devil Hill, near Kitty Hawk, South Carolina

Persuasive Essay

The purpose of a **persuasive essay** is to convince your audience to agree with your position on a specific issue.

Structuring a Persuasive Essay

There are many ways that we influence and are influenced by others. In a formal persuasive essay, however, we try to bring others around to our views by using a defined writing structure. Each part of the structure works with the other parts to present the audience with a clear, compelling case:

- The **position statement** explains what you believe to be true or what you think should be done about a debatable issue. This statement usually occurs in the lead paragraph.

- **Reasons** support your position and explain why you think the way you do. Each reason should occur in its own paragraph. To develop reasons, add the word *because* to your position statement. Then complete the new sentence with a reason that makes an **appeal** that draws the reader into your argument. A logical appeal explains why your position makes sense. An ethical appeal describes why your position is the right thing to do. Finally, an emotional appeal explains why your position will make people feel better about the issue.

- Finally, **evidence** lets your readers know that you have sound support for your ideas.

Note the relationship between the position statement and reasons in the example below. What kind of evidence would support each of these reasons?

Position	More people should adopt pets from animal shelters [*because...*]
Reason 1 (logical appeal)	The variety of animals at a shelter increases the chances that a pet owner will find a good match for his or her lifestyle.
Reason 2 (ethical appeal)	Adopting a pet from a shelter gives an animal a second chance at life.
Reason 3 (emotional appeal)	Pets from shelters become valued friends.

Using a Proper Tone

We often think that people who *argue* are confrontational, combative, or abusive. In a persuasive essay, however, you should argue your case using a reasonable, honest tone. Otherwise you may offend readers who agree with you, as well as those who don't. Which of the paragraphs below is more likely to convince readers of the author's position?

> Our school lunch policy is a bunch of baloney. Why should teachers care if students want to be loud and messy? It's our break time and we totally deserve it.

> The current school lunch policy is too restrictive. Students work hard all morning and by lunch they are ready to blow off a little steam. Granted, rowdiness should be restricted, but giving students a little free time in the middle of the day will make their afternoons more productive.

The first paragraph threatens to offend readers by its confrontational tone. The second paragraph uses concrete, forceful language to make its point. It also acknowledges a possible counterargument without offending people that may have that view. Use a confident, reasonable tone to argue your case, and your persuasive essay is far more likely to produce positive results.

Get Started

You have a right to your opinions, right? That may be so, but an opinion is simply a personal preference, such as "I wish we didn't have to wear school uniforms" or "Homework drives me crazy." An opinion offers your readers no reasons or evidence to help them believe what you claim to be true. Still, you often can use these "knee-jerk" opinions to develop persuasive arguments. Think of a strong opinion you hold. Then ask yourself, "Why should anyone else care?" This will help you to think about the issue from the perspective of your reader, who may share your opinion, but for very different reasons. You can then use this perspective to develop strong, debatable positions, such as "School uniforms do not benefit student performances" and "Homework prevents students from participating in educational opportunities outside of school."

Find Your New Best Friend at an Animal Shelter

When looking for a new puppy or kitten, many people automatically search the newspaper ads or go to a pet store. They might even go to a breeder. Instead, future pet owners should head straight for their local animal shelter, the very best place to find a new best friend.

Pet stores, breeders, and private owners are popular ways to find a new pet. However, each of these suppliers presents risks to animals and to their future owners. For example, pet stores may be convenient, but some store owners care more about profit than about the health and safety of their animals. They often buy animals from "mill" breeders who supply pets cheaply and in large numbers. To meet this large supply, a mill breeder may pair males and females with little thought for whether the resulting babies will be healthy and well tempered.

Beyond the pet stores, many private breeders raise high-quality, purebred animals, but the result is a hefty price tag. Even then, the "best animal" to a breeder will often be one with characteristic physical features. Unfortunately, the breeding processes that produce these features may also shorten the animal's life span or increase instinctual behavioral problems.

Buying animals from strangers out of the newspaper or from the roadside is not a good idea either, because it encourages "backyard breeding." While these backyard breeders often have good intentions, they may not be knowledgeable about what makes a good match of mother and father.

1

Clear position statement

First reason

Evidence

Second reason

Third reason

The best pets come from the local animal shelter. For one thing, the variety of animals at a shelter increases the chances that a pet owner will find a good match for his or her lifestyle. Depending on the size of the shelter, they might have more than just puppies and kittens. Some shelters also have birds, rabbits, hamsters, gerbils, or other legal but unwanted pets. Older animals at the shelter should be considered, as well. These animals are often already house-trained so a new owner won't have to suffer through the pains of training a baby animal.

Fourth reason (appeal to logic)

Furthermore, adopting a pet from a shelter gives that animal a second chance at life. The animals arrive at shelters in various ways. Sometimes a person can no longer keep a pet because of allergies, finances, or a move. Sometimes the pets have been neglected or abused. Whatever its former life was like, adoption from a shelter lets a pet enjoy love and comfort in a new home.

Fifth reason (appeal to right and wrong)

Finally, future pet owners can be assured that the animals they pick from a shelter will be suitable pets. The shelter's staff nurses sick and mistreated animals back to health before they are considered adoptable. An animal with a bad temperament or difficult health problems is not put up for adoption.

Sixth reason (appeal to logic)

Friendship is one of life's greatest joys. Adopt an animal from a shelter and you will gain more than just a pet—you'll gain a happy, healthy new friend!

Conclusion (appeal to emotion)

2

College Entry Essay

"Tell me a little about yourself." That's your task when writing a college entry essay. The purpose of a **college entry essay** is to show a college or university admissions board your personality, charm, talents, skills, and personal vision. In other words, your essay will supply decision-makers with information about you that may not be communicated by your grade point average or your score on a standardized test.

The Application Process

Applying to colleges and universities can require a lot of time and paperwork. Use the hints below to organize your application process and target your essay to the schools that are right for you:

- The first step in writing an effective college entry essay is to decide to which schools you would like to apply. Some people apply to many schools, others to only a few. When you have narrowed your choices, you may want to visit the campus to become more familiar with the school. Also, you can write about the visit in your application entry to show that you already have experience and knowledge about the school.

- Always find out as much as you can about your schools' application procedures and guidelines. Not all schools require an application essay, and those that do may have different criteria for the essay's length and content.

- Do not get too much help from your parents or other adults! Colleges and universities want to know that their students are capable of making informed decisions for themselves. This is especially true when it comes to writing your entry essay. Schools can tell when an essay was written by a professional adult writer rather than a college-bound teenage student. Schools want to see *your* best work, not that of someone else.

Who Are You?

In order to tell another person about your strengths, skills, and outstanding personality traits, you first need to identify them for yourself. Use the process below to show colleges and universities your unique past and promising future:

- Begin by making a list of all your strong points. Are you reliable, generous, intelligent? Can you be trusted? Are you a good friend? List these and other positive traits that you possess. Be honest, but don't be shy!

- Next, think about the significant events in your life, such as those times when you had to step back and assess yourself or your future. Write about something that happened to you that was meaningful or that intrigued you. Write it as a story that excites the reader.

- Ask yourself, "What issues do *I* care about?" Don't ask, "What are *they* looking for?" Admissions boards want a diverse student body that will challenge and support different perspectives. Write something that only *you* could write; use an honest, natural tone.

- Finally, remember, this is not an academic paper! You are writing to introduce yourself to someone. Above all, *be yourself!*

Get Started

When you begin to write your college entry essay, draw on your experience of writing other kinds of essays. For example, a college entry essay contains elements of a narrative essay because you present some aspects of your life rather than a full history. It also contains elements of a persuasive essay, because you generally make a point about some experience or issue and how it affected you. It's also a bit like a letter because you are writing to a defined audience. Pull these elements together with a simple, clear, and direct style. Remember, flowery language won't impress, but being yourself will.

College Entry Essay Example

U.N.C. and Me

When I first stepped foot onto the campus of the University of North Carolina, I fell in love. Majestic tree-lined sidewalks and ivy-covered atriums flanked stately, old colonial buildings that exuded a quiet elegance, unique to the Old South. Having frequently traveled to Virginia and North Carolina to visit my mother's family, I had long ago decided that when I went to college, it would be in the South. Walking across U.N.C.'s campus on this glorious, bright summer afternoon, with all the smells and textures of nature and history filling my senses, I thought, *I am at home. This is where I belong.*

Then, unexpectedly, another thought crept into my mind and burst the bubbles of excitement brewing within me. What if I weren't accepted here? That would be awful!

But wait, I told myself. Be reasonable. You can deal with whatever happens. There have been other times (many times, in fact) when you have not gotten exactly what you wanted, and you lived through it. "Be optimistic, but always be prepared for the unexpected," my mom says. Being a writer, she's no stranger to rejection herself. I realize that if I achieve my goal of graduating with a journalism degree, I too will have plenty of times when my work, and therefore in a sense myself, will be rejected.

I recalled my earliest memory of this painful experience. I was 10 years old, and my best friend had suddenly begun avoiding me. She'd walk the other way when I came into class. Sometimes I saw her quietly whispering to other students, but when I approached them, the conversation would stop. I was heartbroken. My faith in myself and in the whole concept of friendship were shattered.

1

Identify college or university.

Specific details create a story-like "scene" that shows student's knowledge of the school.

Student explains goal (journalism degree).

Personal story and insights reveal author's personality.

Then, a few days later, my friend invited me to her house. When I arrived, there were a dozen people there, among them friends I had recently come to suspect. When they all shouted together "Surprise! Happy Birthday!" my former fears and disappointments suddenly dissolved. If only every uncertain event could have such a happy outcome!

These were my thoughts as I considered my future while standing on the campus that I hoped would soon be my new home. I warned myself that the competition was great. Graduating at the top of my class, scoring great on my SATs, and being involved in lots of extracurricular activities (the French Club, the Yearbook Staff, the Science Fair Committee and Student Council)—these were all assets of "model" students. But I knew there were many such model students. Could I survive a rejection from this school that I so longed to be a part of?

I took a deep breath, looked around again, and resolved to be optimistic but also prepared for the unexpected. Of course, I could survive. Things always have a way of working out for the best, I reminded myself. Either way, I would find myself where I needed to be. So, making one last stop at the Student Union, I bought a sky-blue T-shirt with the U.N.C. logo across the front. I figured it didn't hurt to be prepared for the *best,* either!

2

> **The author stresses strengths in an understated way, while also demonstrating a realistic outlook and an optimistic attitude.**

> **The conclusion reinforces the student's desire to attend the school.**

Letters

With telephones, e-mails, and instant messages, who writes letters anymore? Lots of people still do, including you! The way letters are delivered may have changed, but their purpose and format remains the same. A **letter** is a document that targets a specific person or group, rather than a broad audience. Letters can be handwritten or typed, and sent through the postal service, fax machine, e-mail program, or instant messenger. Use the information below to write letters that effectively communicate your feelings, ideas, and requests to defined audiences.

Personal Letters

Personal letters are written to family and friends. They should be friendly and fun to write. In e-mails and instant messages, the format, language, and even spelling can be informal and filled with personal touches. Keep in mind, though, that your message will fail if the recipient cannot understand what you are trying to say. The following techniques help ensure that your letter's recipients will receive your message "loud and clear":

- In handwritten letters, place the **date** in the upper-right-hand corner of the page. The date is unnecessary when sending an e-mail, as the computer program will supply that information.

- The **greeting** usually begins with the word *Dear,* followed by the recipient's name and a comma.

- In a handwritten letter, **paragraphs** are usually indented and set directly atop each other. If you send your letter by e-mail, separate each paragraph with an empty line and do not indent.

- In a handwritten letter, place the **closing and signature** on the right side of the page. In an e-mail the closing is usually set on the left.

TIME Editors' Tip

While many people use the telephone or e-mail to express their thanks, a handwritten thank-you note in a letter or greeting card is a more personal way to express your appreciation for a gift, a favor, or a job well done. Plus, people always enjoy receiving traditional mail that is not a bill or advertisement!

Sample Personal Letters

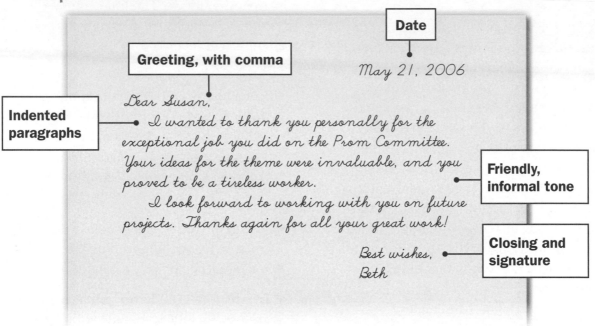

Date

Greeting, with comma

May 21, 2006

Dear Susan,

Indented paragraphs

I wanted to thank you personally for the exceptional job you did on the Prom Committee. Your ideas for the theme were invaluable, and you proved to be a tireless worker.

I look forward to working with you on future projects. Thanks again for all your great work!

Friendly, informal tone

Best wishes,
Beth

Closing and signature

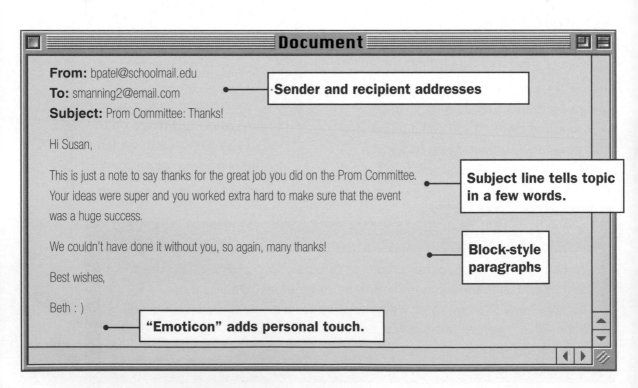

Document

From: bpatel@schoolmail.edu
To: smanning2@email.com
Subject: Prom Committee: Thanks!

Sender and recipient addresses

Hi Susan,

This is just a note to say thanks for the great job you did on the Prom Committee. Your ideas were super and you worked extra hard to make sure that the event was a huge success.

Subject line tells topic in a few words.

We couldn't have done it without you, so again, many thanks!

Block-style paragraphs

Best wishes,

Beth :)

"Emoticon" adds personal touch.

Business Letters

Business letters serve many purposes. You may write a business letter to make a formal request, such as a request for a school transcript or for a recommendation letter. Formal business letter style also is used when writing to public figures or elected officials, or when writing to express an opinion to a newspaper or magazine. All business letters should be neatly typed and state their purpose as briefly as possible, so that they don't tie up too much of the recipient's time. Use the style tips below to communicate effectively with businesses and organizations:

- Place **headers** at the top left of your letter. Include contact information for you and your recipient.

- Use a **greeting** that begins with *Dear*, followed by the recipient's name and a colon. If you do not know the recipient's name, you may address the letter to someone who holds a particular job at the company (Personnel Director, Customer Service Manager) or simply to *Dear Sir or Madam*.

- Use **block paragraphs,** in which the paragraphs are not indented and are separated by an empty line.

- Set the **closing** on the left and use a polite, traditional phrase such as *Sincerely yours,* followed by a comma. Include both a handwritten and a typed signature.

- Always check your letter carefully for grammar and spelling mistakes. Such errors can confuse your message and lead to a delayed or unsatisfactory response.

Get Started

Business letters are more likely to achieve positive results when they are written in a courteous and pleasant tone. When you submit a request, make your point quickly and be sure to thank the recipient for his or her assistance. If you are expressing disagreement or dissatisfaction, you will be taken more seriously if your letter is written in a courteous and respectful way, regardless of your stated opinion.

Business Letter Example, with Envelope

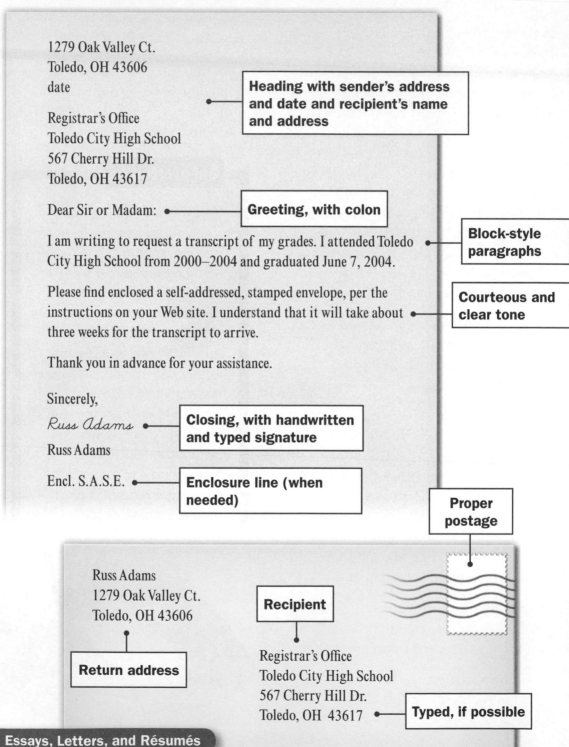

1279 Oak Valley Ct.
Toledo, OH 43606
date

Registrar's Office
Toledo City High School
567 Cherry Hill Dr.
Toledo, OH 43617

Dear Sir or Madam: •——— **Greeting, with colon**

I am writing to request a transcript of my grades. I attended Toledo
City High School from 2000–2004 and graduated June 7, 2004.

Please find enclosed a self-addressed, stamped envelope, per the
instructions on your Web site. I understand that it will take about
three weeks for the transcript to arrive.

Thank you in advance for your assistance.

Sincerely,

Russ Adams

Russ Adams

Encl. S.A.S.E.

Heading with sender's address and date and recipient's name and address

Block-style paragraphs

Courteous and clear tone

Closing, with handwritten and typed signature

Enclosure line (when needed)

Proper postage

Russ Adams
1279 Oak Valley Ct.
Toledo, OH 43606

Return address

Recipient

Registrar's Office
Toledo City High School
567 Cherry Hill Dr.
Toledo, OH 43617

Typed, if possible

Résumés

"I can do this job!" That's the idea that your résumé should convey. A **résumé** is a document that describes your qualifications for a job to a potential employer. A well-written résumé shows that you have the necessary skills or experience for a job and will make you stand out from a crowd of other applicants.

Kinds of Résumés

A résumé is usually your first contact with an employer, so you want it to present your qualifications for a job in an honest but flattering way. Use one of the kinds of résumés below to give employers an accurate, positive picture of your experience:

- The **chronological résumé** is the most common kind of résumé. It lists your employment history in reverse order, beginning with your most recent job. Employers appreciate a well-written chronological résumé because it allows them to see at a glance where else you have worked and for how long.

- But what if you have no prior experience with the kind of job you want? Or you've never held a job at all? You can still shine by

highlighting your special skills in a functional résumé. A **functional résumé** organizes your skills into themes so that an employer can see that you have what it takes to do a job, regardless of your work history. For example, you may have developed strong communication skills by taking on a temporary volunteer position. Or perhaps you have leadership skills from your membership in a school club or sports team.

Get Started ↻

Begin your résumé by gathering all the information you'll need:

Job history: former employer's name, title, phone number, company name, plus your position and responsibilities

Education: schools attended, grade point average (if good)

Volunteerism: contact information for people and organizations

Clubs and teams: memberships and any offices held

Special skills: computer programs, specific tasks

Cover Letter

Always send a brief cover letter with your résumé. A **cover letter** is a one-page business letter that introduces you to the employer and states your understanding of the job. Your cover letter can be more personalized than your résumé, highlighting special skills and indicating why you are interested in the job. Whenever possible, address the cover letter to a specific person at the company.

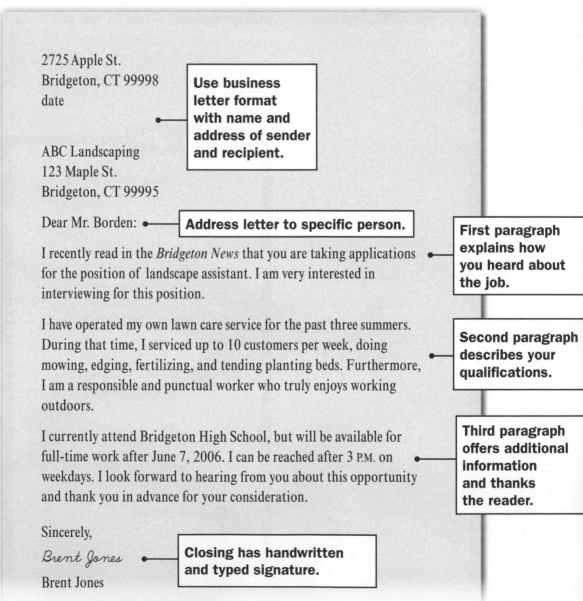

2725 Apple St.
Bridgeton, CT 99998
date

Use business letter format with name and address of sender and recipient.

ABC Landscaping
123 Maple St.
Bridgeton, CT 99995

Dear Mr. Borden: **Address letter to specific person.**

I recently read in the *Bridgeton News* that you are taking applications for the position of landscape assistant. I am very interested in interviewing for this position.

First paragraph explains how you heard about the job.

I have operated my own lawn care service for the past three summers. During that time, I serviced up to 10 customers per week, doing mowing, edging, fertilizing, and tending planting beds. Furthermore, I am a responsible and punctual worker who truly enjoys working outdoors.

Second paragraph describes your qualifications.

I currently attend Bridgeton High School, but will be available for full-time work after June 7, 2006. I can be reached after 3 P.M. on weekdays. I look forward to hearing from you about this opportunity and thank you in advance for your consideration.

Third paragraph offers additional information and thanks the reader.

Sincerely,

Brent Jones

Brent Jones

Closing has handwritten and typed signature.

Chronological Résumé Example

Brent Jones
2725 Apple Street, Bridgeton, CT 99998
(410) 555–4141 • brentjones@email.com

> **Letterhead calls attention to name and contact information.**

Objective
Obtain full-time work in the landscaping industry, providing hands-on assistance in lawn and garden maintenance and implementing landscape designs

> **Objective describes the kind of job you want.**

Work History
2003–2006, Apple Street Lawn Service
Operated independent lawn care service:
* Serviced up to 10 clients per week
* Provided mowing, edging, raking, and leaf-removal services
* Managed own billing, bookkeeping, and advertising using Microsoft Office software

> **Work history lists jobs, beginning with the most recent.**

> **Bullet points draw attention to skills and are easy to read.**

2002–2003, Apple Street Pet Care
Operated independent pet sitting service:
* Cleaned and maintained pet environments for dogs, cats, and birds in owners' homes
* Created and distributed advertising flyers

> **Use parallel structure for phrase in each bullet.**

Education
Currently enrolled at Bridgeton High School

> **Use proper grammar, spelling, and punctuation throughout.**

Awards
Student of the Month, Bridgeton High School, March 2006

References
Available upon request

Functional Résumé Example

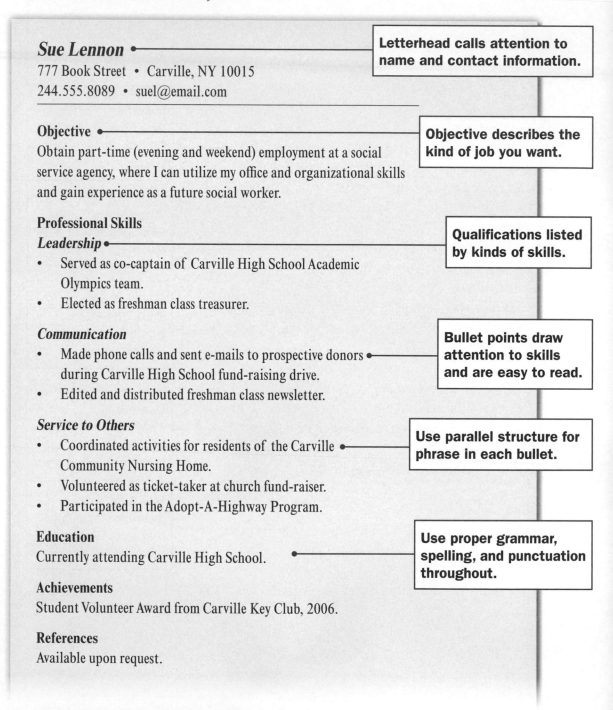

Sue Lennon
777 Book Street • Carville, NY 10015
244.555.8089 • suel@email.com

Letterhead calls attention to name and contact information.

Objective
Obtain part-time (evening and weekend) employment at a social service agency, where I can utilize my office and organizational skills and gain experience as a future social worker.

Objective describes the kind of job you want.

Professional Skills
Leadership

Qualifications listed by kinds of skills.

- Served as co-captain of Carville High School Academic Olympics team.
- Elected as freshman class treasurer.

Communication
- Made phone calls and sent e-mails to prospective donors during Carville High School fund-raising drive.
- Edited and distributed freshman class newsletter.

Bullet points draw attention to skills and are easy to read.

Service to Others
- Coordinated activities for residents of the Carville Community Nursing Home.
- Volunteered as ticket-taker at church fund-raiser.
- Participated in the Adopt-A-Highway Program.

Use parallel structure for phrase in each bullet.

Education
Currently attending Carville High School.

Use proper grammar, spelling, and punctuation throughout.

Achievements
Student Volunteer Award from Carville Key Club, 2006.

References
Available upon request.

Putting It Together: The Writing Process

When you are assigned a writing task, you may feel overwhelmed by the amount of work to be done. You have to find a topic, put your ideas down on paper, and review your work several times before it can be given to your readers. This section of your Writer's Notebook explains how to use a step-by-step process to make writing tasks more manageable. Each step—prewriting, drafting, revising, editing and proofreading, and publishing—builds on the thinking and writing you did in the previous step, until you reach your goal of creating a clear and compelling text for your readers.

The Writing Process

1. **Prewriting**
2. **Drafting**
3. **Revising**
4. **Editing and Proofreading**
5. **Publishing**

Each writer has a different set of skills and ideas, and his or her writing process will reflect that individuality. In fact, there are probably as many versions of the writing process as there are writers. However, even the most creative writers use a step-by-step process to develop their work. There are five common steps in the writing process.

Prewriting is the time to plan and organize your ideas. You will identify the purpose of your writing, brainstorm for a good topic, and then narrow the topic to a manageable size. An organizer, such as a web, can help. Prewriting is also the time to research and organize your ideas. (Section 4 of your Writer's Notebook contains specific suggestions for prewriting a number of common writing assignments.)

Think Again

The step-by-step process is a proven approach to writing, and you should use it regularly. However, sometimes you will need to break out of your usual pattern. For example, while writing a draft you may realize that you need to do more research. At this point, you should return to the prewriting stage to find new information before completing your draft. Remember, a firm process will help you meet deadlines, but a flexible process will help you do your best work.

A proven approach!

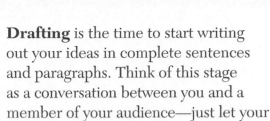

Drafting is the time to start writing out your ideas in complete sentences and paragraphs. Think of this stage as a conversation between you and a member of your audience—just let your thoughts flow as you put them down on paper. (Sections 3 and 4 of your Writer's Notebook present strategies for building paragraphs at the drafting stage, as well as models of complete works.)

Revising is the time to improve your draft by sharing your work with others and receiving their comments. Should you change the structure of your sentences to add variety? Or reorder them to make your ideas clearer? Are your words as precise as they could be? Revising will help you tell your readers exactly what you want them to know. (The first three sections of your Writer's Notebook contain many tips for revising your work.)

Editing and proofreading is when you polish your writing to remove any mistakes that may distract or confuse the reader. You do this by checking spelling, capitalization, punctuation, grammar, and usage. (See also Sections 1 and 2 of your Writer's Notebook.)

Publishing prepares your writing for others to read. During this step, you decide the final format for your work. You may also decide to submit your work to publishers for their consideration.

TIME Editors' Tip

Experienced writers know the importance of reworking their writing until it says just what they want it to say. Here are comments about the writing process from some well-known writers.

"1. Find a subject you care about. 2. Do not ramble, though. 3. Keep it simple. 4. Have the guts to cut. 5. Sound like yourself. 6. Say what you mean to say. 7. Pity the readers."

— *Kurt Vonnegut, novelist and essayist*

"It is better to write a bad first draft than to write no first draft at all."

— *Will Shetterly, writer of novels, screenplays, short stories, and comic books*

"A ratio of failures is built into the process of writing. The wastebasket has evolved for a reason."

— *Margaret Atwood, novelist*

"Books aren't written; they're rewritten."

— *Michael Crichton, novelist, film and television producer*

Before You Write...

You wouldn't wear heavy winter boots during a foot race, would you? Of course not, because they would slow you down or trip you up. And yet, sometimes we get so caught up in thinking about a writing assignment that we forget that writing is a physical activity, too! Take account of the place, time, and supplies you need *before* you sit down to write and you are less likely to get tripped up along the way.

Place. Where do you do most of your writing? In your room? At the dining room table? Many writers become very attached to a particular work setting. Perhaps you like a neat and orderly writing area as a reminder that you should express your ideas in a clear and organized way. Or maybe you like a desk surrounded by books, postcards, and knickknacks that spark your imagination. Whatever the case may be, remember where you do your best work and return to these places regularly during the writing process.

Time. Managing time is one of the writer's most difficult tasks. For some assignments, your teacher may have you work in class or may set deadlines for different stages of your work. Other times, it is your responsibility to see that you set aside enough time to complete an assignment. To do this, pay attention to how well your mind and body function at different times of day. Some writers work best in the mornings, when they are fully rested and their minds are fresh. Others prefer to get the day under way before they approach an empty page or revise a draft. Set aside time for writing during the most productive part of your day to increase your chances of success.

Supplies. Think about the supplies you need to complete your work well before a writing assignment is due. Notebook paper for prewriting, printer paper for drafts and final submissions, an erasable pen or pencil for revisions, a stapler for longer essays—keep these items handy at home or be sure you know where they can be found in your school.

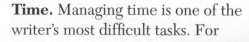

1 Prewriting

Think of the prewriting step as laying a foundation for your work—just as a building needs a solid base, your essays, letters, and résumés need solid thought and planning. In **prewriting**, you think about what you are going to write, choose a topic, research information, and organize the material.

Know Your Purpose

So, where do you begin? It starts with your **purpose**. Your teacher may define the purpose of a writing assignment, or you may choose to write because you have a story or message to share.

Always pay attention to the directions for an assignment or the prompt on an essay test, because this information will help you define your purpose. If the assignment is an expository essay, you should give information about the subject. For example, you might give information about the causes of the Civil War. If you are assigned a persuasive essay, then your purpose is to convince the audience to agree with your position on an issue, such as the importance of conserving energy. To write a descriptive essay, you should depict a person, place, or event, such as a story about the antics of your pet cat. Below are some purposes for writing and the forms they can take:

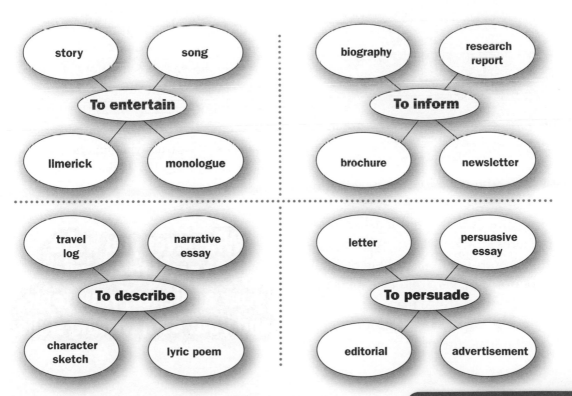

The Writing Triangle

Whenever you write, you need to consider your audience, your topic, and your own writing skills. Think of this relationship as a triangle. All three points in the triangle must work together to create a successful piece of writing. For example, if you write about a subject you find boring, it will show in your writing. The reader will no doubt be bored, too, and you will not do justice to the topic. If you write with enthusiasm, your audience will read with interest, and your topic will receive the attention it deserves.

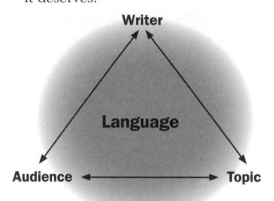

Consider some possible audiences and subjects. The audience for expository writing often will be your teacher and classmates. You may be assigned to write an expository essay about any number of subjects, from an explanation of how the Gold Rush played a part in westward expansion to information about the structure of an atom. However,

sometimes the audience for expository writing extends beyond the classroom. A written explanation for a friend who asks how to send a photo by e-mail is expository writing, too.

The audience for a persuasive essay often will be a teacher, but it also may be the general public through publication in a newspaper's or magazine's "letters to the editor" section. The topic of a persuasive essay or letter is an issue about which you feel strongly and for which there is some disagreement, such as global warming or proposed changes to the length of the school year.

Your class or a club to which you belong may have a newsletter. If you contribute to it, your audience is the group who reads the newsletter. The topic is probably a special event or a person who has recently done something noteworthy. Whatever your writing assignment may be, you as the writer must consider how you relate to each part of the writing triangle and how these parts relate to each other.

Whenever you write, you need to consider your audience, your topic, and your own writing skills.

Idea Development

Where do writers get their ideas? From the world around them, of course! What you experience, others experience, too. Through writing, you can communicate with others about common ideas and experiences. The following six pages present a number of techniques for engaging with the world around you, and turning those experiences into focused writing topics.

Observe

Idea development begins when you are actively engaged with the world. Even life's ordinary moments can provide ideas for the observant writer.

Experience the World. Take a walk. Ride your bike to the mall. Watch the shoppers and wander through the food court. Keep your eyes open and notice things that you usually take for granted. Wonder about what you see, hear, smell, touch, and taste. Ask yourself questions:

- Why are there so many different breeds of dogs?
- Is there such a job as an ice cream taste-tester?
- Why do doughnuts have holes?

Be an Active Viewer. Watch the news on television or read a newspaper. Take in a movie or an art exhibit. But don't just sit there passively. Ask yourself these questions to be an active viewer:

- How do I feel about this event or artwork?
- How does a fictional or real-life story affect *my* life?
- Is there anything I can do about an event or its effects?
- What's my opinion on this debate? Do I need more facts before I can form an opinion?

TIME Editors' Tip

Writer Julius Lester was asked where he gets ideas for his books. He said, "I don't get ideas as much as I get a feeling and want to know more about that feeling. I spend a lot of time wondering what it's like to be someone I see on the street, or what it was like to have been alive at a certain time in history, or what it's like to have something happen to you. Writing comes as much from the heart as it does from the head."

66

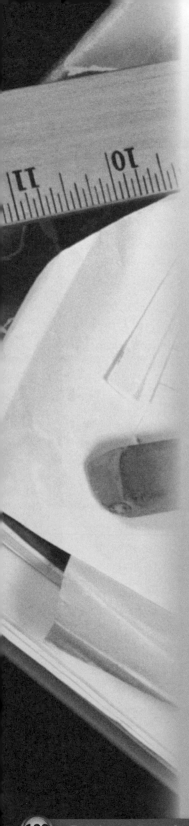

Read

Read, read, and then read some more! Reading helps you develop a sense of how ideas are communicated, and it provides you with models of good writing.

Read Anything, Anytime. It matters less what you read than that you read regularly and think about the texts in front of you. Newspapers, Web sites, and magazines are widely available and can address almost any topic that interests you. *The key to becoming a good writer is to keep reading!*

Visit a Library or Bookstore. Browse the shelves to see the different categories of books. Are you more interested in science fiction or true adventure stories? Be sure to check out the shelves of best sellers—what are people reading about these days? Use the library's or bookstore's online catalog to see which books are available about a topic that interests you.

Go Online. On the Internet, a world of information is only a few keystrokes away. Use the Internet to visit libraries, bookstores, and other information sources around the world. Use a search engine to identify magazines or blogs about your interests. When you find a great site, share it with your friends so they can read along with you!

Investigate Encyclopedias. Read short articles in an encyclopedia at your library. They can stir your curiosity and help you choose a topic, or they can help you discover new ideas about an assigned topic. Encyclopedias also are available on the Internet. You may be able to access an online encyclopedia at your library.

Use Your Textbooks. Textbooks can give you topic ideas for many kinds of writing assignments. Scan the table of contents and the index for subjects that grab your interest. If the text has a glossary, you may find a word that suggests a topic. If the textbook has a bibliography—a list of other related works—you may be able to use some of the listed books and articles to begin your own research.

Write

Writing, like any skill, becomes easier with practice. Remember, not everything you write has to be polished prose. You can learn about how your own mind uses language by writing ideas in a casual, loosely organized way. Below are some techniques you may want to try.

Journals, scrapbooks, and blogs are an excellent way to practice your writing skills and collect possible topics for future writing assignments. There are many ways to create a journal or scrapbook. Some people write in notebooks about daily events or ideas from their personal lives. Other people write about a specific topic, such as soccer, dance, or the environment. Many writers also post their thoughts on the Internet in Web logs, or "blogs." Like scrapbooks, blogs often allow writers to post images along with their texts.

Letters and e-mails give you the chance to practice writing to a specific audience, usually one person but sometimes a group. E-mail also allows you to save copies of your work in one place, usually a software program or Web site. Thus, you can easily find and reread your old e-mails to track how your writing skills have changed.

Freewriting means to write for 5 to 10 minutes about a topic without stopping. Just jump right in and start writing! Don't take time to go back and correct anything. If you can't think of anything to write, then write about your lack of ideas. Sometimes ideas only come when you start putting down words.

Directed dialogue is a written conversation about your topic between two people: yourself and a pretend member of your audence. Use freewriting to create the dialogue. Ask yourself:

- What questions would this person have about the topic?
- How would I answer those questions?
- What information would I need to look up to find or support my answers?

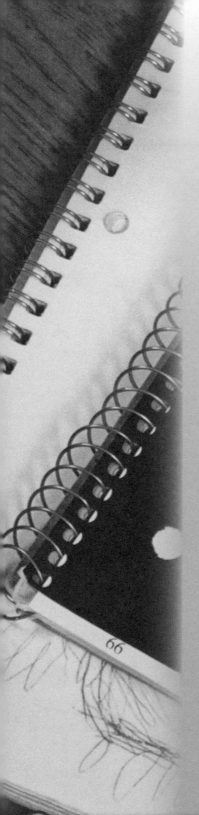

Ask

Questions are one of the most powerful tools in a writer's tool kit. Like a sharp saw blade, questions cut deep into ideas and experiences and turn them into material for strong written works. Use the techniques below to hone your questioning skills.

Ask "What If...?" The way things are isn't always the way things have to be.

- What if your ancestors had never come to America?
- What if we made college tuition free for everybody?
- What if a character in your favorite novel had acted differently?

Questions like these challenge you to think about your life in strange and interesting ways. They help reveal the people, places, and events that lie hidden behind everyday appearances. Ask "What if...?" to let your mind's eye peer into a whole new world of possibilities.

Ask Others. Don't be afraid to ask others to help you with your work. You'll probably approach your teachers first, but there are many friendly people who know a lot about writing and enjoy helping others. Librarians are experts at finding books and articles about a wide range of subjects. Many authors are happy to respond to questions about their work and share their own tips for successful writing. Whether you ask in person or in writing, approach your "helpers" politely and state your questions as clearly as possible,

Listen Up! When you pose a question to yourself or to others, always pay close attention to the response. A question is only useful when you are open to its answer. Take notes if necessary. If you do not understand an answer, follow up with a more specific question. Remember, questions are like saws—they only work when moving back and forth!

Choose a Topic

After you have gathered topic ideas from your reading, writing, and other experiences, how do you choose the best one? Recognizing good writing ideas is as much a skill as is using a computer or performing ballet. As you consider topics, ask yourself the following questions:

- **Does the topic accurately fulfill the assignment?** Writing your life story isn't a good idea if your teacher has assigned a research report. If you are assigned a compare-contrast essay, you'll want a topic that allows you to show similarities and differences.
- **Do I already have information about this topic?** If you have some experience or knowledge about a topic, you probably have already given it some thought. A lightly blazed trail is better than no trail at all when you are deciding on a topic.
- **Is this topic interesting enough that I want to learn more about it?** If you are writing a report or formal essay, you may have to work on your topic for a long time. You'll want to choose a subject that will keep your interest.
- **Is this topic something others have written about?** If others have written about your topic, you will have materials to use for research or as models. Also, the fact that others have written about a topic is a clue that it is of interest to others. Finding out who these people are will help you discover the audience for your writing.
- **Will I learn something new as the result of my work on this topic? Am I likely to find something new to share with my audience?** Through writing, you will change and grow, and you will help others do so, too. People read to learn about their world. They will read what you write if it offers new information, insight, or even just a fresh way of discussing a topic.

Narrow It Down

Writing assignments can take several forms. Sometimes you are given a broad topic and then asked to focus on one aspect of it. Other times you may choose any topic you want. In either case, zoom in on your topic to make your writing process manageable and your final paper readable. Consider the techniques for narrowing topics for the following kinds of assignments:

Write an expository essay about the wonders of nature. There are many, many wonders in nature. To begin narrowing the topic, list a few questions, such as those below. Decide which one most interests you and then do some research to discover if enough information is available. As you work, you may find you need to narrow your topic even more.

- What causes hurricanes?
- Why is acid rain a problem?
- Why have black rhinos become endangered?
- What is an asteroid?

Write a persuasive essay on an issue that affects your school. Here you must select a topic related to a problem or concern at your school, but you still have some say in just what that topic will be. Perhaps you want to write about a menu change in the cafeteria or a new dress code. Carefully think through how you feel about the issue because you'll need to take a clear position on it. Brainstorm a list of reasons to support your argument.

Write a research report on any subject. The freedom to choose can make getting started even more difficult. Begin by writing a list of things that interest you. Suppose you look at your list and choose architecture. You still need to find a clearer focus. You might write about one type of building and give examples (airport terminals or skyscrapers), or you might compare two styles of homes (the Prairie style and the Queen Anne style). The important thing is to choose a focus that you will enjoy researching and communicating to others.

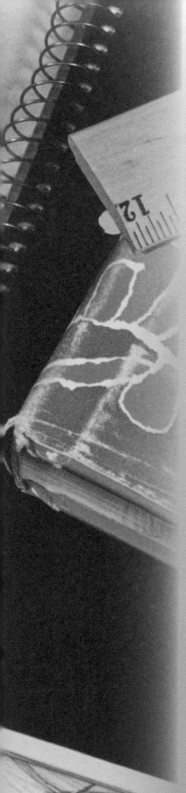

Graphic Organizers

After you have chosen a topic, it's time to start organizing your ideas. Use the graphic organizers on the following pages to "give shape" to your ideas.

A **web** is a wonderfully flexible way to see relationships among different ideas. Suppose your topic is the ecology of wetlands. Write the topic in the center circle or oval. Then write related subtopics in the ovals around the center. Details can be jotted down in ovals that branch off from the subtopics.

Five W's and an H refers to questions news reporters ask to make sure they have covered the important points in a story. You can create a graphic organizer to ask the same questions about your topic. You may have to do some research to find answers to every question. Below is an example of how this graphic organizer can help you write an expository essay about the Declaration of Independence.

Who?	Thomas Jefferson wrote the Declaration; Congress revised it.
What?	A document declaring the American colonies independent of Great Britain
When?	July 4, 1776
Where?	Philadelphia, Pennsylvania
Why?	Colonists didn't want to pay taxes to Great Britain or be ruled by a king.
How?	The Continental Congress passed the Declaration. The first public reading was on July 8. On July 19, Congress ordered it to be signed by members.

Who?
What?
When?
Where?
Why?
How?

A **Venn diagram** helps you compare and contrast information. Place individual aspects in the individual circles. Place shared aspects in the area where the circles overlap.

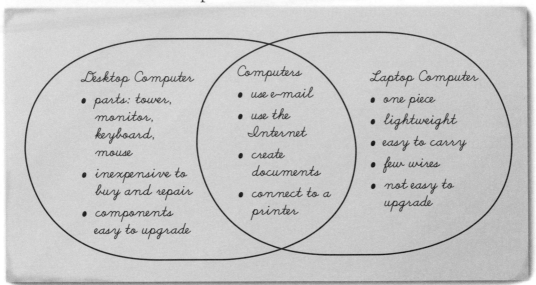

Desktop Computer
- parts: tower, monitor, keyboard, mouse
- inexpensive to buy and repair
- components easy to upgrade

Computers
- use e-mail
- use the Internet
- create documents
- connect to a printer

Laptop Computer
- one piece
- lightweight
- easy to carry
- few wires
- not easy to upgrade

A **cause-and-effect chart** shows relationships between actions. In such charts, either the cause or the effect may be given first. Keep in mind that one cause can lead to more than one effect. Other times, an effect has more than one cause.

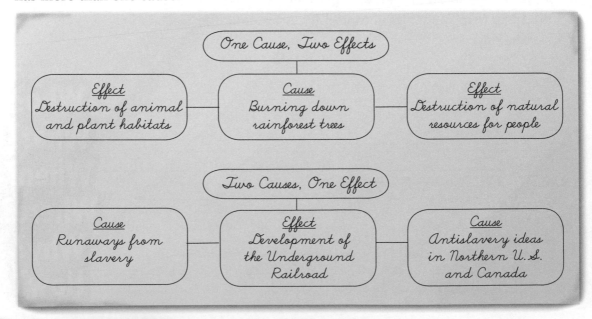

One Cause, Two Effects

Effect
Destruction of animal and plant habitats

Cause
Burning down rainforest trees

Effect
Destruction of natural resources for people

Two Causes, One Effect

Cause
Runaways from slavery

Effect
Development of the Underground Railroad

Cause
Antislavery ideas in Northern U.S. and Canada

A **time line** helps you present events in the order they occurred. Use a time line when writing personal narratives, biographies, and histories.

Time Line for Biography of Ellen Ochoa			
Born in Los Angeles	Graduated from San Diego State University	Became first Hispanic woman astronaut	Won NASA's Exceptional Service Medal
1958	1980	1991	1997

A **pro-con chart** helps you state a problem and discuss the benefits and risks of various solutions.

Problem	Solution	Pros	Cons
Homelessness	Job training, affordable housing	People have work and can pay for housing	Taxes need to be increased to provide training and housing

A **how-to chart** presents steps for doing something in order. These charts are especially useful when you want to write directions for a science experiment or instructions for a game.

Activity: Develop a New Game	Purpose: Challenge Your Memory
Step 1. Put 20 small items (comb, key, etc.) on a tray. Cover with a cloth.	
Step 2. Players sit in a circle with tray in center.	
Step 3. Remove the cloth for 1 minute and then replace it.	
Step 4. Each player writes the names of as many objects as possible.	
Step 5. Uncover the tray and name the objects.	
Conclusion: Players check answers. Player with the most correct items wins.	

Outlines

An **outline** is a tool for organizing your work into main ideas and details. An outline also provides you with a kind of "checklist" of items to include in your draft. Outlines can take several different forms.

A **scratch outline** consists of words or phrases jotted down to remind you of the ideas they represent. Scratch outlines are very flexible, but they usually list in order the ideas you want to present in your work. These outlines work well for essay tests and other assignments written in class.

1. How hurricanes form

2. Hurricanes becoming more powerful

3. In recent years, more Category 4 and 5 hurricanes

4. Global warming?

A **topic outline** includes more detail than a scratch outline. Write the main idea in a complete sentence in the heading. Then organize your main ideas and details using indented numbers and letters in the following order: Roman numerals, capital letters, standard numerals, lowercase letters. Follow each number or letter with a word or phrase.

I. Introduction: Hurricanes, which form over oceans and bring destruction when they strike land, may be becoming more powerful.
II. How hurricanes form
   A. Over the ocean
   B. In areas of low pressure
      1. Draw in air
      2. Circling winds
   C. Air warmed by the heat of oceans and rises
      1. Intensifies
      2. Heavy rainfall
III. Hurricanes becoming more powerful
   A. Ranked by strength in 5 categories
      1. Category 1 weakest
      2. Category 5 strongest
   B. Category 4 and 5 hurricanes
      1. More from 1990–2004 than 1975–1990
      2. More in all the oceans

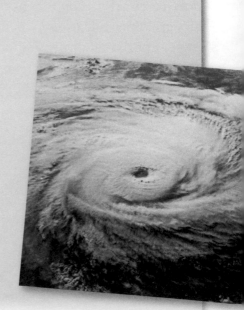

A **sentence outline** has the same format as the topic outline, but includes complete sentences. Each item should contain only one fully punctuated sentence. Use this type of outline to force yourself to think through the ideas and fill them out a bit. Often the sentences you use in this outline can be used as the thesis and topic sentences in your full draft!

I. Introduction: Hurricanes, which form over the ocean and bring destruction when they strike land, may be becoming more powerful.

II. In the northern hemisphere, hurricanes form over water from June 1 until November 30.
  A. They form over the ocean, especially where the waters are warm.
  B. They begin in areas of low atmospheric pressure.
    1. The growing storm draws in air from surrounding areas of high pressure.
    2. The winds circle counterclockwise in the northern hemisphere, due to the earth's rotation.
  C. Air warmed by the oceans rises through the storm.
    1. Further warming causes the storm to intensify.
    2. High winds, heavy rainfall, and flooding may result.

III. Hurricanes may be becoming more powerful than in the past.
  A. Hurricanes are ranked in 5 categories.
    1. Category 1 hurricanes are the weakest and may damage shrubs and signs.
    2. Category 5 hurricanes are the strongest and may destroy nearly everything in their path.
  B. Category 4 and 5 hurricanes are becoming more common.
    1. There were more Category 4 or 5 hurricanes between 1990 and 2004 than 1975 to 1990.
    2. These more powerful hurricanes occurred in oceans around the world.

TIME Editors' Tip

Always pair the items in an outline. In other words, if there is a I, there must be a II. If there is an A, there must be a B. You can have more than two items, but not fewer. This ensures that your readers will receive the depth and breadth of information they need to understand your topic.

2 Drafting

Now you're ready to start writing! Instead of trying to produce a perfect copy, use a series of **drafts** to develop your ideas. At this stage, don't worry if your writing is rather rough. After all, revising is the next step.

Beating Writer's Block

It is easy to put off getting started with your draft, but that's a mistake. "Writer's block" is a common problem, and there are several effective techniques for working through it. Try these hints if you can't get started:

- Review the notes you made during the prewriting step.

- Get up and walk around to clear your head.

- Use one of these openers to get started: a quotation, a question, an anecdote, a statement of opinion, a startling fact, or an analogy.

Remind yourself that it helps just to start writing. Often you won't really start working until you have something to work with—putting the first words on paper gives you something concrete to build on and refer back to. Once you get some ideas down on paper, you can go back and add or delete ideas later. Try to write as much as possible of your first draft in one sitting, while ideas are fresh in your mind. Write with your natural voice, on paper or on a computer—it doesn't matter where. *Just start writing!*

TIME Editors' Tip

Always save your original draft, whether on paper or a computer! You may want to go back to something in your original during the revising step. When you compose on a computer, be sure to protect your work by using the "save" command often. Computers can and do experience technical problems.

Formatting Your Draft

Use the format below to provide space for comments and revisions on your draft. (You can use a similar format for handwritten drafts.)

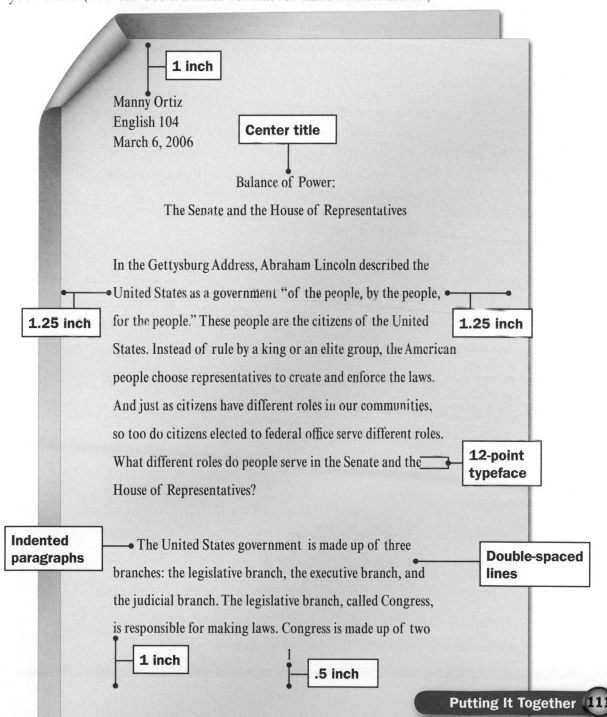

1 inch

Manny Ortiz
English 104
March 6, 2006

Center title

Balance of Power:

The Senate and the House of Representatives

In the Gettysburg Address, Abraham Lincoln described the United States as a government "of the people, by the people, for the people." These people are the citizens of the United States. Instead of rule by a king or an elite group, the American people choose representatives to create and enforce the laws. And just as citizens have different roles in our communities, so too do citizens elected to federal office serve different roles. What different roles do people serve in the Senate and the House of Representatives?

The United States government is made up of three branches: the legislative branch, the executive branch, and the judicial branch. The legislative branch, called Congress, is responsible for making laws. Congress is made up of two

1.25 inch

1.25 inch

12-point typeface

Indented paragraphs

Double-spaced lines

1 inch

.5 inch

3 Revising

After you have completed a draft, it's time to make it stronger by revising. When you **revise** your draft, focus on how the paragraphs, sentences, and words organize and communicate your message. Keep in mind that you may have to revise your work several times.

Paragraphs

Paragraphs give structure to your ideas and organize them in a coherent way. Each paragraph should have a single point, or main idea. Each sentence in a paragraph should explain or illustrate this main idea. In a well-organized text, each paragraph flows smoothly into the next. Notice the revisions below. The writer has moved the topic sentence, cut an irrelevant sentence, and added a transitional phrase.

Rough Draft

Unlike fossil fuels, which have a limited supply, renewable fuel sources can be planted and harvested repeatedly. These fuels are often made from widely cultivated *In fact* crops. ~~In 1979 President Jimmy Carter gave his "Crisis of Confidence" speech about the energy problem.~~ Renewable fuels are a possible answer to our long-term energy needs. Soybeans and sugarcane have already been blended with gasoline to create new fuels. Some engines can even be made to run on used vegetable oil.

Revised

Renewable fuels are a possible answer to our long-term energy needs. Unlike fossil fuels, which have a limited supply, renewable fuel sources can be planted and harvested repeatedly. In fact, these fuels are often made from widely cultivated crops. Soybeans and sugarcane have already been blended with gasoline to create new fuels. Some engines can even be made to run on used vegetable oil.

Sentences

Examine your essay sentence by sentence and ask the questions below.

Is the wording ambiguous or incomplete? When something is ambiguous, it has more than one possible meaning. Revise ambiguous sentences to say exactly what you mean.

Ambiguous	Clear
Martin said he would call me on Tuesday.	Martin will call me next Tuesday.
Carol knows more students than Liz.	Carol knows Liz and many other students.

Is the pronoun reference clear? When you use pronouns, make sure readers can identify which noun the pronoun represents.

Unclear	After removing the stereo from his car, Jeff sold it.
Clear	Jeff removed the stereo before selling his car.
	Jeff sold his car stereo.

Is the sentence too wordy? Your writing will be stronger and easier to read if you don't use more words than are necessary.

Wordy	Maria did not pay attention to the fact that she had failed.
Concise	Maria ignored her failure.

Does the text include clichés? Clichés are worn-out expressions that weaken your writing. Avoid them.

sly as a fox	rotten to the core	sell like hotcakes
fresh as a daisy	easy as pie	nick of time

Is there nonstandard language? Some expressions that you may use when speaking are not used in standard writing.

Nonstandard usage	He don't even know chemistry, so whatever.
Standard usage	He never studied chemistry, so ignore him.

Words

Depending on your assignment, your draft may contain hundreds or even thousands of words. Every one of these words gives your audience a small piece of information about your topic and about you as a writer.

Be Accurate, Be Expressive

Many students believe that research papers and other formal essays require leaden, boring writing. Not true! Note how different words add interest and style to the fact-based sentences below.

Dry	Internet video game players are a growing group.
Expressive	Online gamers are a flourishing subculture.

Dry	Architect Frank Gehry has built many famous buildings all over the world.
Expressive	Master builder Frank Gehry has crafted many notable international projects.

Each of the dry sentences presents an idea clearly and grammatically. And yet the words are so well-worn that readers may wish that the writer had conveyed his or her ideas more expressively. The expressive sentences have the same sentence structure as the dry originals, but they use vivid verbs and interesting nouns to enhance the text's meaning and readability. When you revise your work, search for places to do the same. Don't overdo it, though! Keep a dictionary and thesaurus handy to ensure that your words are accurate as well as expressive.

TIME Editors' Tip

"A rose is a rose is a rose," writer Gertrude Stein once said. "I think in that line the rose is *red* for the first time . . . in a hundred years." Repeating a key word can make complicated ideas easier to understand or drive home an important point. Note the impact of the repeated words below:

"**Love is** patient; **love is** kind; **love is** not envious or boastful or arrogant or rude." — *St. Paul*

"**I** came, **I** saw, **I** conquered." — *Julius Caesar*

Troubleshooter

Fun Fixes

When it's just not working…when your back is against the wall… sometimes you have to think "outside the box." Use the techniques below to break out of your ordinary writing habits.

Picture This. Student writers often complain that they know what they want to say, but they don't know how to say it. So don't say it! Cut out images and blocks of text that relate to your topic from old magazines and newspapers. Use the cutouts to create collages that communicate your ideas in a new way. Then rework your ideas by describing your artwork and explaining what it is trying to say.

Cut and Paste, for Real. In the days before computers, writers and editors actually cut and pasted paper text blocks to create printed pages. Today's word-processing programs allow you to do the same thing much more quickly. However, when your eyes have grown weary of staring at a computer screen, sometimes the old ways work best. Print out a copy of your draft and use a scissors to cut out each paragraph. Now you can move paragraphs like pieces in a jigsaw puzzle and try out new combinations and relationships. When you have locked the pieces into place, return to the computer and make the edits to your digital document.

Become a Stranger to Yourself. Some students will always say, "I'm not a very good writer." So become someone who is! One writer puts on a tie when he revises his work to remind himself that he is doing serious business. Another writer will read her work aloud in a fake accent so the words will sound different and new. These techniques are a bit silly, but they work.

Am I Done Yet? An Essay Checklist

Essays are the most common form of student writing. And although there are many kinds of essays, every essay should contain certain elements. If you cannot find the elements below in your essay or you cannot answer yes to each question, return to the appropriate section of your Writer's Notebook and use the information and examples there to revise your work.

Title
Circle the title of your essay.

> ✔ Is your title centered on the first page of your essay?
> ✔ Does the title describe your topic accurately, yet expressively?

Lead
Draw a line between your lead and the body paragraphs.

> ✔ Does your lead occur at or near the very beginning of your essay?
>
> ✔ Is your lead paragraph separate from the other paragraphs?

Place a star next to the sentence(s) in the lead that "hook" the reader.

> ✔ Does your hook occur early in the lead paragraph?
> ✔ Does your hook relate to the topic?

If you have written an expository or persuasive essay, underline the thesis sentence.

> ✔ Does your thesis sentence occur at the end of the lead paragraph?
> ✔ Does the thesis sentence clearly state your topic or position?

Body Paragraphs
Number in order each of your body paragraphs.

> ✔ Do you have at least three body paragraphs?
> ✔ Are the paragraphs of a reasonable length— neither too short nor too long?

Underline the topic sentence in each paragraph.

- ✔ Does each topic sentence clearly tell the reader what the paragraph is about?
- ✔ Does each sentence in the paragraph relate to the topic sentence's main idea?

Circle the transitional words and phrases in each paragraph.

- ✔ Do the transitions in the paragraph's first sentence link to the previous paragraph?
- ✔ Are there a variety of transitions linking the sentences within paragraphs?

Conclusion

Draw a line between your body paragraphs and your conclusion.

- ✔ Is your conclusion separate from other paragraphs?
- ✔ Is your conclusion at the very end of your essay?

Place a star next to the sentence(s) that refer back to the lead paragraph.

- ✔ If you used a quote in your conclusion, does it relate to another quote in the lead?
- ✔ If you used a summary sentence, does it restate the ideas in the lead's thesis sentence?

Works Cited

Circle the Works Cited heading in your essay.

- ✔ Does your Works Cited page occur at the very end of your essay?
- ✔ Did you indent lines after the first line in each entry?

Circle the first word in each Works Cited entry.

- ✔ Are the entries alphabetized by the author's last name or the first major word in the title?
- ✔ Does each entry use the proper MLA style?

Place a small box next to each entry. Review your work and place a check mark in the box when you find the matching citation in the text.

- ✔ Did each Works Cited have a matching citation in the text?
- ✔ Did you find any citations in the text whose source was not listed in the Works Cited?

Does my essay contain these elements?

Check!

4 Editing and Proofreading

Editing and proofreading give your text a final polish before you present it to your readers. To **edit** your work, check for correct grammar in sentences and proper usage of words. Then **proofread** your work to identify and fix errors in spelling, mechanics, and punctuation. The tips below will help you perform this detailed work effectively:

- **Keep distractions down.** It's difficult to search out stray letters and commas when a stereo or television is competing for your attention. Move to a quiet, well-lit room to do your final editing and proofreading.

- **Use an erasable pen or pencil.** You may have to correct your corrections! After all, nobody's perfect.

- **Read one line at a time.** It often helps to place a ruler or folded piece of paper beneath each line as you read. This technique keeps your eyes trained on a single line of text. You also can use it to mark your place if you need to take a break or ask someone else's opinion.

- **Don't overdo it.** If you get bogged down second-guessing your work, you will never complete your assignment. Note any problems with your earlier work in the writing process and remember them for next time. There will always be more opportunities to write!

- **Keep your Writer's Notebook handy.** This book is designed to help you find solutions to common writing problems quickly and accurately. Keep it close by during your editing and proofreading stage and you'll feel as if there's a writing teacher at the table with you, guiding your work.

TIME Editors' Tip

In the publishing business, before a book is printed it may go to a **cold reader.** This is someone who has not participated in any way in the writing or editing of the book. The cold reader's job is to find those mistakes that everyone else has missed. Think of the people you know. Do any of them have the editing skills to become your cold reader?

Self-Editing

The ability to identify and fix problems in your work is one of the most important skills a writer can have. It also can be one of the most difficult to do well. After spending so much time developing one's ideas and putting them into words, writers often have great difficulty seeing their text through the readers' eyes. Use the following techniques to help you identify areas of improvement in your draft:

- **Print a hard copy to read.** Your readers will probably read a paper copy, and you should, too.

- **Put your draft aside and then read it "cold."** When you leave time to put your work aside, you will return to it with a fresh perspective.

- **Read the draft aloud.** Some things look good on paper but sound odd when spoken aloud. You can read the draft to yourself, to someone else, or have someone else read it to you.

- **Read it more than once.** You won't catch all the problems in only one reading. Don't even try!

Peer Editing

In peer editing, you work with a partner or group to improve your writing. This is an especially valuable part of the revising process because others will often catch different mistakes than you will find in your own work. The tips below will help you and your writing partners work together to improve each others' work:

- **Read carefully.** Don't rush through the text.

- **Speak thoughtfully.** The point of peer editing is to help your partners improve their work, not criticize or make fun of them.

- **Offer specific examples.** It doesn't help much to say, "You aren't using capital letters correctly." Instead, say, "The word *Philadelphia* should begin with a capital letter because it is the name of a city."

- **Offer solutions.** Providing specific solutions to problems not only helps your partners, it helps you sharpen your own writing skills.

Proofreaders' Marks

Proofreaders' marks are symbols that help you identify and correct problems in your essay. Even when you compose on a computer, it is useful to print a copy that you can mark up. Don't trust the spell-check or grammar-check functions on your computer. They will miss many errors. For example, they probably won't catch the word *their* used in place of *there*. Then return to the computer to make your finished copy.

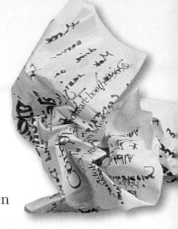

Mark	Action	Mark	Action
∧	Add letter or word	⌣	Close up space
℘	Remove letter or word	≡	Capitalize
#	Add space	/	Lower case
∧	Add comma	*ital*	Italicize
⊙	Add period	¶	Start new paragraph
∨	Add apostrophe	*tr* ⌐	Transpose (switch)
∨ ∨	Add quotes	*stet*	Stet (let it stand)
∴ ∵	Add colon/semicolon	sp	Correct spelling error

Sometimes called the Red Planet Mars was named for the ~~Roman~~ god of *stet* war⊙ It got its nickname because it is a reddish object in the nightsky. Its the fourth Planet from the Sun, after Mercury, Venus, and Earth. Two robots named *ital* Spirit and Opportunity were launched from cape canaveral in Florida. Both landed on Mars in January of 2004 and set off to investigate the rocks and soil *tr* of Mars. They went in search later of clues to find out if parts of Mars may at sp one time have been a sutible place to support life.

4 Publishing

This is it—you're almost done! Like a marathon runner nearing the finish line, you've come a long way and the end is in sight. But before you're truly finished, there's one more important step to take. **Publishing** is when you decide how you will share your work with others. Take care during this step to present your audience with the clear and readable results of all your hard work.

Publishing Homework

Your teachers and classmates are the most frequent audience for your work. Use the hints below to show them the quality of your thinking and writing:

- **Page Format.** For most writing assignments, format your pages using the information on page 110 of your Writer's Notebook. As in your early drafts, you want to give readers plenty of room to write corrections and comments on your final copy. That's how you'll learn!

- **Writing Folders.** Students are often asked to submit their papers in folders that contain examples of the work they did at each stage in the writing process. Whenever you write, be sure to keep any materials that illustrate how you developed your work, from prewriting through to publication.

- **Writing Portfolios.** A writing portfolio is a collection of your best work. Sometimes you will be required to submit a writing portfolio for class or as part of the admissions process for a college or university. You may also want to develop a portfolio on your own in order to track your progress as a writer. Either way, prepare a Table of Contents page for your portfolio that lists the titles of your works. Also, write a brief introduction page that describes your writing skills and how each piece in the portfolio contributed to their development.

Think Again

Publishing does not always mean preparing a printed paper copy of your work. Giving a speech, creating a poster, or building a multimedia presentation are other ways to present your work to others. Ask your teacher if you may use these forms to replace or support your traditional writing assignments.

"Four score and seven years ago..."

Publishing Beyond the Classroom

There are few things more satisfying than seeing one's own words in print. Publishing your work outside the classroom exposes your work to the responses of a much larger readership and will help you gain confidence in your writing skills. When you have a piece of writing that you feel strongly about, consider submitting it for publication to the outlets below:

- **School Publications.** Many schools have publications by and for their students. Find out how you can get involved with your school newspaper or yearbook as a reporter, columnist, or editor. Other schools publish a collection of student writing called a review. Take advantage of these or other opportunities to reach readers in your learning community.

- **Local Newspaper.** People of all ages and writing abilities submit letters to the editors of daily newspapers. Usually these are persuasive letters about an important issue in the community. Also, some newspapers have special sections about young people or the world of education. Such sections may publish student essays and fiction writings on a particular theme.

- **Young Adult Publications.** There are many publications and Web sites that feature the writing of young writers. Ask your writing teacher or librarian about good online outlets for your work.

- **Writing Contests.** Contests are a fun way to develop your writing skills. Some contests ask for essays about a particular theme. Others may ask you to write a story based on a set opening line. Whenever you enter a contest, pay close attention to the guidelines for the topic, length, and due dates. Remember, if you don't enter, you can't win!

Troubleshooter

After You Write...

Student writers are busy writers—sometimes you barely have time to complete one writing task before you begin another one. Other times you may have to juggle many writing tasks at the same time. Take time after major writing assignments to evaluate your growing skills as a writer. The questions below will help you develop a clearer sense of where your writing skills are and where you would like them to be.

What was the easiest part of the writing assignment? Do you come up with a number of good topics when you prewrite an essay? Are you a good editor or proofreader? Different writers excel at different parts of the writing process. Knowing which parts you are especially good at will increase your confidence and therefore your chances for success. You can use your strongest skills to help others improve their writing, too. Remember, nobody is good at everything, but everybody is good at something.

What was the most difficult part? Some writers have difficulty achieving the proper length in their works. Others struggle to pull paragraphs together in a satisfying way. When you know your weaknesses, you know when you will most need to focus your energy. You will also have a better sense of when to ask for help.

What did I learn about my topic? Most writing teachers ask you to consider your audience carefully when you write, but don't forget that your own intellectual development is important, too. At the end of a writing assignment, you should have learned something important or useful about your topic.

What will I do differently next time? The opportunity to develop your ideas is built into the writing process, but that opportunity is not fully realized if you repeat the same mistakes or rely on the same strengths for every writing assignment. For good writers, revising is not a single step in a process—it's a way of life!

Index

A

Abbreviations, 35
   commas in, 38
Acronyms, 35
Active voice, 12
Adjectives, 6, 15
   comparative/superlative, 15
Adverbs
   comparative/superlative, 16
America (Baudrillard), 70
The American Teenager (Burns), 70
Answers (Yes/No/Maybe)
   commas in, 38
Apostrophes, 41
Appositives, commas in, 37
As I Lay Dying (Faulkner), 28
"At the Crossroads," 58–59
Atwood, Margaret, 95
Audience, 98, 103, 121, 123
Audio-visual media, 66
Author, 63
   identifying, 61, 69

B

Baudrillard, Jean, 70
"Best Books for Young Adults
   2005," 71
Body paragraphs, 65, 72
   body builders in, 49–50
   topic sentences in, 47, 73, 112,
      116–17
   transitions in, 48, 74, 117
Books, 66
   Works Cited page entries for, 70
Bullets, 39
   for chronological résumés, 91
   for functional résumés, 92
Burns, Kate, 70
Bush, George W., 68
Business envelope
   postage for, 88
   recipient of, 88
   return address for, 88
Business letters, 87–88
   enclosure line for, 88
   example of, 88

   style tips for, 87
   tone of, 87–88

C

Capital letters, 22, 95
Cause and Effect Charts, 106
Characters, 56
Chronological résumés, 55, 89, 91
Citations, 65, 67, 72, 73, 75, 117
   how to use, 69
   when to use, 68
Clauses
   dependent/independent, 27
Clichés, 113
Cohen, Herman, 71
Cold readers, 118
College entry essay, 54, 81–84
   application process and, 81
   example of, 83–84
   identifying skills/traits and
      strong points for, 82, 84
Colons, 39
   for greetings, 88
Commands, 26, 35
Commas, 36–38, 120
   for greetings, 86
Communication, 5
Complex sentence, 28
Compound personal pronouns, 14
Compound sentence, 28
   commas in, 36
Compound-complex sentence, 28
Conclusions, 51–52, 65, 68, 75, 84,
   117. See *also* Signature/closing
Conjunctions, 17, 22
Cooper, B. Lee, 70
Cover letters, 55, 90
"Creep" (Radiohead), 71
Crichton, Michael, 95
Current events essay, 64

D

Dashes, 42
Dates/numbers, 24, 85, 86
   commas in, 38
   in letters, 85, 86
Definition essay, 64

Descriptive essay, 97
Dialogue, 56, 59
   Directed, 101
Directed speech, commas in, 37
Documentation. See *also* Citations;
   Works Cited page
   citation as, 65
   Guide, 68–71
   Works Cited page as, 65
Drafting, 93, 94, 95, 110–11
   format for, 111

E

Editing/proofreading, 93, 94, 95,
   118–20, 123
   marks for, 120
   peer, techniques for, 119
   self, techniques for, 119
   tips for, 118
Ellipses, 41
E-mail, 55, 85
   paragraphs/closing in, 85
   sample of, 86
   writing practice in, 101
"Emoticon," 86
Encyclopedias, for writing ideas,
   100
Essays, 53. See *also* College entry
   essay; Current events essay;
   Definition essay; Descriptive
   essay; Expository essay;
   Historical essay; Literature
   response essay; Narrative essay;
   Persuasive essay; Process essay
   checklist for, 116–17
   examples for, 45
   kinds of, 54
   understanding ideas of, 61, 63
Evidence, 61, 63, 65, 77, 79
Examples
   using in essays, 45
Exclamations, 26
   commas in, 38
   punctuation for, 35
Expository essay, 54, 64–76, 97,
   104, 116, 117. See *also* Citations;

Current events essay; Definition
   essay; Documentation;
   Historical essay; Process essay;
   Works Cited page
   elements of, 65
   example of, 72–76
   kinds of, 64
   note-taking for, 67
   research for, 66
   topics for, 65

F

Faulkner, William, 28
Fiction techniques. *See also*
   Narrative essay
   characters as, 56
   plot as, 56
   setting as, 56
"Find Your New Best Friend at an
   Animal Shelter," 79–80
Five W's and an H, 105
Fragments, fixing, 30
"Frantic Lives Trigger Teen
   Depression" (Kampert), 71
Freewriting, 101
Functional résumés, 89, 92

G

Gallagher, Laura A., 70
Gerunds, 9
Get Started
   on business letter's tone, 87
   on expository essay topics, 65
   on librarians, 66
   on narrative essay subjects, 57
   on opinions, 78
   on prewriting, 60
   résumé information to, 89
   on writing assignments, 55
   on writing experience, 82
Grammar, 95, 118
   for business letters, 87
   for résumés, 91, 92
   rules for, 6
Graphic organizers, 105–7
Greetings
   for business letters, 87, 88
   for letters, 85, 86
   punctuation for, 38, 86, 88

H

Headers
   for business letters, 87, 88
   for cover letters, 90
   for e-mail, 86
Hemingway, Ernest, 28
Hines, Thomas, 69
Historical essay, 64
Homework
   University of Michigan research
   on, 61
"The Homework Ate My Family"
   (Ratnesar), 61
How-to Charts, 107

I

I Want That! (Hines), 69
I Was a Teenage Werewolf, 71
Idea development, 99–104, 123
   observation for, 99
   reading for, 100
Indefinite pronouns, 14
Infinitive form, 10
"Inside the Teenage Brain," 71
Intensity, word choice influencing,
   7
Interjections, commas in, 38
Internet, 64, 66
   sources on, 71
Interpretation
   evidence for, 61, 63
   structural/stylistic, 61, 63
Interviews, 66
Italics
   for emphasis, 23
   for foreign words, 23
   names/titles in, 23
   for specific terms, 23

J

Job history, 89–91
   in chronological résumés, 91
Journals/scrapbooks/blogs
   writing practice in, 101
Joyce, Colin, 71

K

Kampert, Patrick, 71
Kenny, Maureen E., 70

L

Lead paragraphs, 44–46, 65
   hook for, 116
Lester, Julius, 99
Letterhead
   in chronological résumés, 91
   in functional résumés, 92
Letters, 53, 85–88
   business, 55
   personal, 55, 85–86
   writing practice in, 101
Librarians, 66, 102
Library/bookstore
   location, 67
   for writing ideas, 100
Listening, 102
Literature response essay, 54,
   60–62
   elements of strong, 61
   example of, 62–63
   kinds of, 60
Locations/addresses, commas in, 38
Loesch, Rebecca, 71

M

Marsalis, Wynton, 62–63
Meaning, word choice influencing,
   7
Mechanics, 20, 118
Media, Works Cited page entries
   for, 71
Merged sentences. *See also* Run-on
   sentences
   punctuation in, 29
"The Message of New Orleans," 63
Modern Language Association
   (MLA), 68, 71, 76, 117

N

Narrative essay, 54, 56–59
   example of, 58–59
   fiction techniques for, 56
   sensory descriptions for, 57–58
New Orleans, 62–63
Newspapers, 122
Nonstandard language, 113
Note-taking, 67
Noun cases
   gerunds for, 9
   kinds of, 9

Nouns, 6, 8–9, 59
  collective, 8, 11
  common, 8
  proper, 8
Numbers, 24, 74
Numerals, 24

O

Object noun cases, 9
Object pronoun cases, 13
Objective
  in chronological résumés, 91
  in functional résumés, 92
Observation, for writing ideas, 99
The Old Man and the Sea
  (Hemingway), 28
Outlines, forms of, 108–9

P

Page format, 121
Palladino, Grace, 70
Paragraphs, 43, 72, 112, 123
  body, 47–50, 65, 72, 95
  for business letters, 87, 88
  to compare/contrast, 50, 74
  for cover letters, 90
  for drafting, 111
  for e-mail, 85–86
  lead, 44–46, 52, 65, 116–17
  in letters, 85, 86
Parallel structures, 31
  in chronological résumés, 91
  for functional résumés, 92
Parentheses, 42
Participles, present/past, 10
Passive voice, 12
Past tense verbs, 11
Periodicals, 66
  Works Cited page entries for, 71
Periods, 35
Personal Letters
  parts of, 85
  sample of, 86
  tone in, 86
Personal pronouns, 14
Persuasive essay, 54, 77–80, 97,
  104, 116
  evidence in, 77, 79
  example of, 79–80
  position statement in, 77, 79
  reasons in, 77

structure of, 77
tone of, 78
Phrases
  commas for beginning, 37
  commas for unneeded, 37
  descriptive, 27
  subject, 27
Plot, 56, 58–59
"Popular Music Reflects Teens'
  Attitudes About School"
  (Cooper), 70
Possessive noun cases, 9
Possessive pronoun cases, 13
Predicate, 27
Prepositions, 17, 22
Present perfect tense verbs, 10
Present tense verbs, 10
Prewriting, 60, 93, 94, 123
  knowing purpose for, 97
Process essay, 64
Pro-Con Charts, 107
Pronouns, 13
  antecedents for, 13–14
  cases of, 13
  kinds of, 14
Publishing, 95
  beyond classroom, 122
  homework, 121
Punctuation marks, 95, 118. *See
  also* Apostrophes; Colons;
  Commas; Dashes; Ellipses;
  Exclamations; Greetings;
  Merged sentences; Parentheses;
  Periods; Questions; Quotations;
  Semicolons; TIME Editors'
  Tips purposes of, 34–42

Q

Qualifications
  in cover letter, 90
  for functional résumés, 92
Questions, 26
  listening and, 102
  punctuation for, 35
  reader related, 45
  skill in, 102
  as writer's tool, 102
Quotations, 45, 65, 67, 68, 72, 75,
  117
  commas for, 37
  direct/indirect, 40

identifying, 69
punctuation for, 40
secondhand, 69, 73
for titles, 40, 72, 116
for tone change, 40

R

Radiohead, 71
Ratnesar, Romesh, 61
Reasons/appeals, 79
  emotional, 77, 80
  ethical, 77, 80
  logical, 77, 80
Relative pronouns, 14
Research, 66
  report, 104
Résumés, 53, 89–92
  chronological, 55, 89, 91
  cover letter for, 55, 90
  functional, 55, 89, 92
  kinds of, 89
Revising, 93, 95, 112–15, 123
  examples of, 112
*The Rise and Fall of the American
  Teenager* (Hines), 69
Rules
  grammar, 6
  usage, 6, 95, 118
Run-on sentences, 29

S

"Saving America's Soul Kitchen"
  (Marsalis), 62
School publications, 122
Scratch outlines, 108
Semicolons, 39, 120
Sentence outlines, 109
Sentences, 25–30, 95, 113
  fragments, 30
  kinds of, 26
  length of, 32
  outline, 109
  parts of, 27
  run-on, 29
  structure of, 28, 33, 95
  varying, 32–33, 95
Setting, 56
Shakespeare, William, 40
Shetterly, Will, 95

Signature/closing
  for business letters, 87, 88
  for cover letters, 90
  for letters, 85, 86
Simple sentence
  compound predicate with, 28
  compound subject with, 28
Sources, 65–71. See also Citations;
  MLA; Works Cited page
  alphabetical order for, 70, 76,
    117
  library, 67
  noting all, 67, 70
  variety of, 66
Spelling, 20–21, 95, 118
  for business letters, 87
  for résumés, 91, 92
  spell check for, 21, 120
Statements, 26, 35
Statistics, 45
Style, word choice and, 7
Subheadings, 65, 72, 73
Subject, 27
Subject noun cases, 9
Subject pronoun cases, 13
Subject-verb agreement, 11

T

Table of Contents, 121
Teenagers: An American History
  (Palladino), 70
Teenagers and Community Service:
  A Guide to the Issues (Kenny,
  Gallagher), 70
Textbooks, for writing ideas, 100
Thesis sentences, 46, 47, 51, 65,
  109, 116, 117
Think Again, 7, 13, 23, 45
  on bullets, 39
  on collective nouns, 11
  on commas, 36
  on fragments, 30
  on gerunds, 9
  on lead paragraphs, 46
  on periods, 35
  on prepositions, 17
  on publishing, 121
  on step-by-step process, 94
TIME Editors' Tips, 6, 8, 12, 14,
  15, 19, 26, 33, 47
  on capitalizing, 22

  on citations, 69
  on "cold readers," 118
  on conclusions, 51
  on digressions, 49
  on drafts, 110
  on ellipses, 41
  on exclamation points, 35
  on getting ideas, 99
  on modifiers, 16
  on numerals, 24
  on outlines, 109
  on parallel structures, 31
  on participles, 10
  on publishing, 122
  on punctuation, 34
  on sentence structure, 28
  on sources, 71
  on spelling, 21
  on titles, 44
  on traditional letters, 85
  on transitions, 48
  on writing process experience,
    95
  on writing triangle, 54
Time lines, 107
Titles, 22–23, 40, 44, 58, 63, 72,
  111, 116
  identifying, 61
Topics, 65, 94, 98, 123
  choosing, questions for, 103
  narrowing, 104
  outlines for, 108

U

"U.N.C. and Me," 83–84

V

Venn Diagrams, 106
Verbs, 6, 10–11, 57, 58
  tenses, 10–11
Voice
  active, 12
  passive, 12
Vonnegut, Kurt, 95

W

Wallis, Claudia, 71
Webs, 105
Webster's Ninth New Collegiate
  Dictionary, 70

"What Makes Teens Tick" (Wallis),
  71
The Wizard of Oz, 68
Word choice, 7, 95
  dry, 114
  of nouns, 8
Wordiness, 7, 113
Words, 5
  ambiguous/clear, 113
  commonly misspelled, 21
  commonly misused, 18–19
Works Cited page, 65, 67, 76, 117
  creating, 70–71
  entries for, 70–71, 76, 117
Wright, Orville, 72–75
"The Wright Stuff: The Wright
  Brothers and the First
  Airplane," 72–76
Wright, Wilbur, 72–75
Writer's block, 110, 115
Writer's Notebook, 5, 25, 43, 53,
  93, 118, 121
Writer's skills, 98
Writing
  for assignments, 55, 96, 103,
    104, 108, 121, 123
  contests, 122
  to describe, 97
  to entertain, 97
  folders, 121
  idea development for, 101
  to inform, 97
  to persuade, 97
  portfolios, 121
  preparation for, 96
  process of, 93, 94–95
  questions after, 123
  student, 54, 123
Writing triangle, 54, 98

Y

Young adult publications, 122

Traits of Good Writing Index

Ideas
asking, 102
business letters, 87
choosing a topic, 103
college entry essays, 81–82
idea development, 99–104
literature response essays, 60
narrative essays, 57
narrow a topic, 104
observing, 99
persuasive essays, 77–78
reading, 100
research, 66
résumés, 89
writing, 101

Organization
body paragraphs, 47–50
expository essay, 64–65, 72–76
graphic organizers, 105–107
lead paragraph, 44–46
letters, 85–88
literature response essay, 60–61
note-taking, 67
outlines, 108–109
persuasive essay, 77–80
plot, 56
résumé, 89–92
revising paragraphs, 112
revising sentences, 113

thesis sentences, 46
topic sentences, 47
transitions, 48
persuasive essay, 77–80
Works Cited page, 70

Voice
active, 12
in business letters, 87
in college entry essays, 82
in lead paragraphs, 44
passive, 12
in persuasive essays, 78
writing triangle, 98

Word choice, 7
adjectives, 15
adverbs, 16
commonly misused words,
    18–19
conjunctions, 17
nouns, 8–9
prepositions, 17
pronouns, 13–14
purple prose, 16
revising words, 114

subject-verb agreement, 11
verbs, 10–11

Sentence Fluency
clauses, 27
fragments, 30
kinds of sentences, 26
parallelism, 31
parts of sentences, 27
phrases, 27
predicates, 27
punctuation, 34–42
subjects, 27
revising sentences, 113
run-ons, 29
sentence structures, 28, 33
variation, 32–33

Conventions
capitalization, 22
college entry essay, 81–84
documentation guide, 68–71
expository essay, 64–76
essay checklist, 116–117
forms of writing, 54–55
italics, 23
letters, 85–88
literature response essay, 60–63
mechanics, 20
narrative essay, 56–59
numbers, 24
persuasive essay, 77–80
proofreading, 120
spelling, 20–21

Presentation
of drafts, 111
of homework, 121
for publications, 122